How to Use
THE WORLD WIDE WEB

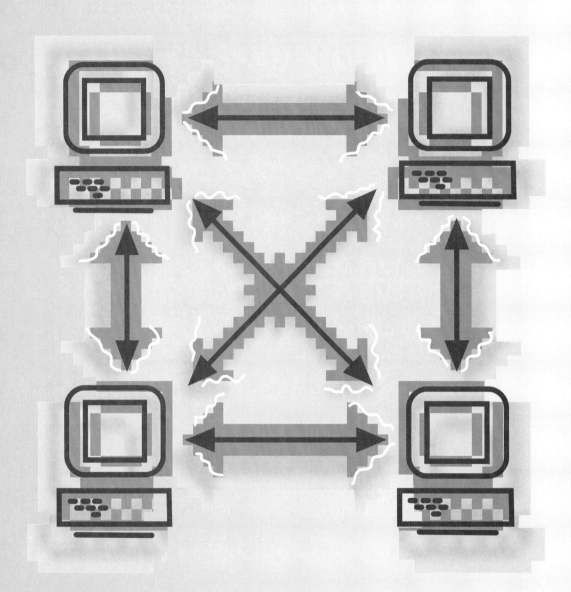

How to Use
THE WORLD WIDE WEB

WAYNE AUSE AND SCOTT ARPAJIAN

Ziff-Davis Press
an imprint of Macmillan Computer Publishing USA
Emeryville, California

Development Editor	Kelly Green
Copy Editors	Kim Haglund and Margo Hill
Technical Reviewer	Mitzi Waltz
Project Coordinator	Barbara Dahl
Cover Illustration	Megan Gandt
Cover Design	Regan Honda
Book Design	Dennis Gallagher/Visual Strategies, San Francisco
Technical Illustration	Sarah Ishida
Word Processing	Howard Blechman
Page Layout	Janet Piercy
Indexer	Valerie Robbins

Ziff-Davis Press, ZD Press, and the Ziff-Davis Press logo are trademarks or registered trademarks of, and are licensed to Macmillan Computer Publishing USA by Ziff-Davis Publishing Company, New York, New York.

Ziff-Davis Press imprint books are produced on a Macintosh computer system with the following applications: FrameMaker®, Microsoft® Word, QuarkXPress®, Adobe Illustrator®, Adobe Photoshop®, Adobe Streamline™, MacLink®Plus, Aldus® FreeHand™, Collage Plus™.

Ziff-Davis Press, an imprint of
Macmillan Computer Publishing USA
5903 Christie Avenue
Emeryville, CA 94608
510-601-2000

Copyright © 1996 by Macmillan Computer Publishing USA. All rights reserved.
PART OF A CONTINUING SERIES

All other product names and services identified throughout this book are trademarks or registered trademarks of their respective companies. They are used throughout this book in editorial fashion only and for the benefit of such companies. No such uses, or the use of any trade name, is intended to convey endorsement or other affiliation with the book.

No part of this publication may be reproduced in any form, or stored in a database or retrieval system, or transmitted or distributed in any form by any means, electronic, mechanical photocopying, recording, or otherwise, without the prior written permission of Macmillan Computer Publishing USA, except as permitted by the Copyright Act of 1976, and except that program listings may be entered, stored, and executed in a computer system.

THE INFORMATION AND MATERIAL CONTAINED IN THIS BOOK ARE PROVIDED "AS IS," WITHOUT WARRANTY OF ANY KIND, EXPRESS OR IMPLIED, INCLUDING WITHOUT LIMITATION ANY WARRANTY CONCERNING THE ACCURACY, ADEQUACY, OR COMPLETENESS OF SUCH INFORMATION OR MATERIAL OR THE RESULTS TO BE OBTAINED FROM USING SUCH INFORMATION OR MATERIAL. NEITHER MACMILLAN COMPUTER PUBLISHING USA NOR THE AUTHOR SHALL BE RESPONSIBLE FOR ANY CLAIMS ATTRIBUTABLE TO ERRORS, OMISSIONS, OR OTHER INACCURACIES IN THE INFORMATION OR MATERIAL CONTAINED IN THIS BOOK, AND IN NO EVENT SHALL MACMILLAN COMPUTER PUBLISHING USA OR THE AUTHOR BE LIABLE FOR DIRECT, INDIRECT, SPECIAL, INCIDENTAL, OR CONSEQUENTIAL DAMAGES ARISING OUT OF THE USE OF SUCH INFORMATION OR MATERIAL.

ISBN 1-56276-392-X

Manufactured in the United States of America
10 9 8 7 6 5 4 3 2 1

TABLE OF CONTENTS

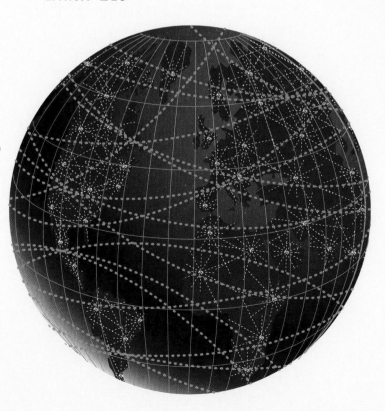

ACKNOWLEDGMENTS

 This book is the culmination of a tremendous odyssey and adventure not unlike the process of catching a tiger by the tail. It took countless hours of wrangling to get a grasp on the ever-changing and fiercely dynamic Web environment.

Kelly Green, Development Editor at Ziff-Davis Press, gets much of the credit for helping to tie this beast down. Barbara Dahl, Suzanne Anthony, and Kim Haglund, also with Ziff-Davis, get high marks as well for keeping this book on track. And thanks to my co-author, Scott Arpajian, who like the calvary rode to the rescue and gave this book the push it needed to get from concept to reality.

I would also like to acknowledge the kindness of friends, relatives, and supporters: my top-notch agent, Karen Nazor; Christopher Hughes; Neal Ause; Mitzi Waltz; Stephen Schultz; and Lenny Charnoff.

This effort would not have been possible without the generosity and patience of the many contributing Web site designers and companies featured in this book. I would also like to thank the thousands of people who helped me without even knowing it just by contributing helpful information and resources to this primordial soup called the Web.

And, of course, I wish to thank my beautiful wife Kendra Hogue for her limitless faith and patience, and my little boy Carter for occasionally interrupting me to remind me about the important things in life.

—Wayne Ause

For her persistence, patience, encouragement, and friendship, Kelly Green at Ziff-Davis Press deserves a surplus of thank-yous. I'd also like to acknowledge my friends and co-workers for putting up with me during a very hectic few months. Nancy O'Brien, Peter Kim, Dave Marden, Tim Rempe, Tim Smith, Erik Kokkonen, Chris Faust, Ken Hart, and many others were all there when I needed them.

Thanks, guys.

—Scott Arpajian

INTRODUCTION

 Separating fact from fiction and hype from hypertext can be a challenge these days when you consider the sheer amount of "buzz" currently circling about the Internet.

One thing is for certain: The development and growth of the Internet represents a global communications revolution. No one can accurately predict where it's going and when (or if) it will end. We can only guess where it will take us, even with thousands of visionaries hard at work plotting the new roadmaps to this frontier.

For the first time in history, you, your relatives, neighbors, and friends all have relatively easy access to a communications medium that is global, immediate, and multidirectional. Not only can everyone see what others are saying and doing at any time anywhere in the world, but also people can contribute to the mix—they can toss in their own stories, ideas, experiences, and anything else that can be translated into the digital language of computers.

This book helps guide the reader to a wildly popular and very powerful piece of the Internet puzzle—the Web. It will help you delve into the intricacies and jargon of the Web environment. It will also provide you with a look at pages created by designers who have helped blaze the Web trail.

From pointers to key Web sites, to an exploration of the developing technologies driving and changing Web activity, to basic rules of the road, this book will help keep you on course in your travels through the ever-expanding information superhighway.

If you have any questions or comments, send us e-mail. We'd love to share your ideas and concerns with the rest of the people we bump into every day out in cyberspace.

—Wayne Ause
wause@aol.com

Scott Arpajian
Scott_Arpajian@ZD.com

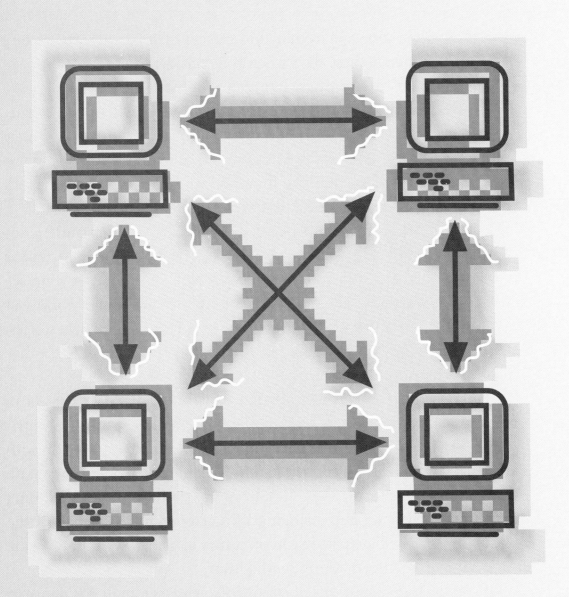

CHAPTER 1

How the Web Works

Everyone is talking about the World Wide Web. It's on TV, it's all over the newspapers—it seems as though every week the media is buzzing about the latest thing happening on the Web. Even the more traditional commercial online services such as America Online and CompuServe are joining the frenzy as they scramble to provide access and services for browsing and publishing on the World Wide Web.

The reason for this frenzy is that the Web is exciting. Electronic communications and computers are changing the way we do everything, and the Web is acting as a catalyst, both speeding up the process and shaping it at the same time.

Using the Web, you can communicate with a large number of people (conservatively estimated to be over 30 million and rising rapidly), you can find resources for information on every topic, and you can spend hours swimming through the full spectrum of human creativity, ingenuity, imagination, and levels of silliness that you never knew existed before. In short, it's not just important, popular, and useful—it's also a heck of a lot of fun.

This chapter will explain what the Web is, what it can do, and how it works—a tall order for one little chapter but a worthy goal. These are all important topics to touch on before we discuss how to use the Web.

What Is the Internet?

The World Wide Web is part of the Internet. The Internet is a huge collection of computer networks that can communicate with each other—a network of networks. And a network is a collection of interconnected, individually controlled computers. Through networks, each computer user can communicate and share common resources, such as printers and storage space, with other users. The Internet is built upon thousands of smaller regional networks spread out around the world. Roughly 30 million users in over 50 countries plug into the Internet through these smaller networks each day.

TIP SHEET

▶ Internet access providers (also called Internet service providers, or ISPs) are commercial services that establish a connection to the Internet and then provide public access to that connection for a fee. ISPs often also provide a host of other Internet-related services such as technical support, free software, and the option of storing personal information in directories and files on their computers.

▶ ISPs usually connect to the Internet through special high-speed phone lines that can carry much more information than a standard telephone line. The number and the capacity of the high-speed lines operated by the ISP determines how many subscribers they can service.

❶ A *network* consists of two or more computers that are connected to each other and share a common computer language enabling them to communicate. The Internet takes this concept further by interconnecting many of the largest computer networks around the world. When you connect to the Internet from work or home, your computer becomes a small part of this giant network.

❹ Now new networks are connecting to the Internet each day. In recent years, hundreds of new Internet access providers have started providing low-cost connectivity to the general public. And all the major commercial online services now provide Internet access for their customers.

2 The first computers to form the Internet were connected to major U.S. government and Department of Defense networks. The purpose was to establish a reliable method for disseminating information in the event of a national emergency.

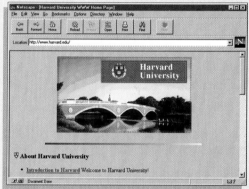

3 Soon more computer networks joined the Internet as people got excited about the possibility of one large system for sharing information and accessing databases. Most of these new Internet users were at major colleges, universities, and research institutions around the world.

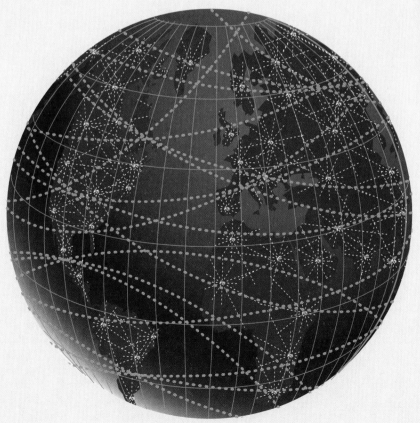

How Does the Internet Work?

I t takes more than a physical connection between two computers to make a network. Networks function because they use a common language to communicate over those connections. The common language of the Internet is called *TCP/IP*, which stands for *Transmission Control Protocol/Internet Protocol*. Every computer on the Internet agrees to communicate using this language.

1 Because all computers on the Internet agree to use TCP/IP, it doesn't matter what kinds of computers are in place or what operating software each machine is running. For example, a Macintosh can communicate with a PC or UNIX-based machine.

TIP SHEET

▶ **No single network known as "The Internet" really exists. Instead, regional networks such as SuraNet, PrepNet, and FidoNet are interconnected into a single monster entity, communicating at amazing speeds with the TCP/IP protocol.**

▶ **Other networks such as UUCP (Unix-to-Unix Copy Program) and BITNET (Because It's Time Network) are not as large as the Internet, but are also loose associations of "subnetworks" like the Internet that communicate using common language protocols. These networks are used primarily by researchers and large commercial entities. Because they don't use the TCP/IP protocol, these networks are not considered part of the Internet. But people on these networks can send e-mail and exchange data with people on the Internet through gateways.**

4 Since the Internet doesn't really exist as a defined physical entity, there is no single place to call and complain or to send money for access. Each of the regional networks that make up the Internet supports its own operation independently. This process works well to ensure the viability of the whole in that if one network goes down, the rest of the Internet will remain operational.

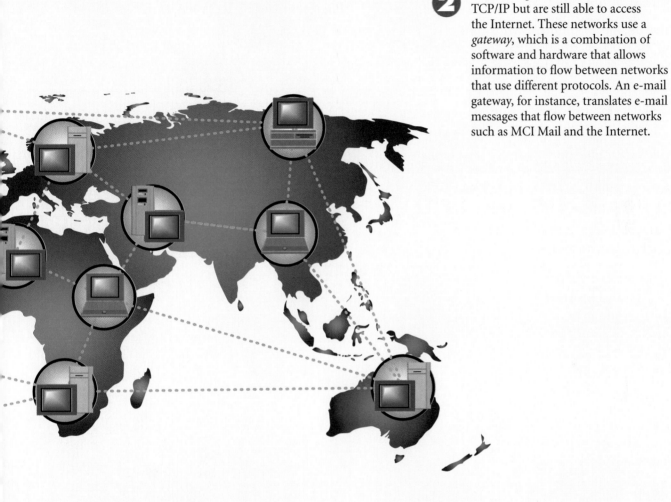

2 Some computer networks don't use TCP/IP but are still able to access the Internet. These networks use a *gateway*, which is a combination of software and hardware that allows information to flow between networks that use different protocols. An e-mail gateway, for instance, translates e-mail messages that flow between networks such as MCI Mail and the Internet.

3 The Internet is governed by "consensual anarchy," which means that no one is in charge of the whole thing. Some of the smaller networks that plug into the Internet have governing bodies, but no one person or group oversees the entire Internet.

How Does the Web Fit In?

A common misconception is that the World Wide Web is the same thing as the Internet. In fact, it's not. Even though nearly every aspect of the Internet is accessible with a Web browser, the *Web* refers to a specific kind of Internet interface; one that uses hyperlinks and multimedia documents. The Internet, on the other hand, refers to the physical side of the global network, a huge collection of computers and cables. And the Internet offers much more than just Web resources. Here are all the major pieces that make up the Internet.

World Wide Web

▶ **1** The Web is the largest and fastest growing part of the Internet. For most people, it is the easiest to use, but it does have limitations that are not found in other parts of the Internet. The main limitation is speed. It often takes much more time to view a graphical Web page than it does to access any of the other Internet offerings.

Usenet News Groups

6 *Usenet* is a massive collection of news and discussion groups on the Internet. These public forums attract postings that range from the extreme to the extremely boring and are full of debate, pleas for help, helpful (or insulting) answers, and gossip.

TIP SHEET

▶ Another increasingly popular aspect of the Internet is IRC, or Internet Relay Chat. IRC is the CB radio of the '90s, allowing users to communicate in real time via their keyboards over the Internet. IRC uses different channels to allow for separate discussions.

▶ Other popular activities on the Internet include live audio and video conferencing. Through the use of special hardware and software, you can use the Internet to communicate face-to-face with anyone around the globe.

E-mail

2 *E-mail*, short for *electronic mail*, is still the most used and highly developed aspect of the Internet. E-mail allows the user to easily send and receive personal messages or participate in mass-mailing lists. Even most networks that don't yet have full TCP/IP access to the Internet do provide e-mail gateways. Most of the larger commercial online services started with e-mail access before upgrading to full Internet connectivity.

File Transfer Protocol

3 *FTP* stands for *File Transfer Protocol*, which allows users to easily transfer files between computers on the Internet and their home computers. FTP sites are often vast storehouses holding such digital treasures as shareware, freeware, demo applications, multimedia files, and plain text-based information. Anything that can be put into a digital format can be transferred on the Internet via FTP.

Gopher

4 *Gopher* is an application based on the concept of clients and servers. Clients are programs used to request information; servers are programs that provide the requested information to the clients. Gopher servers are all over the Internet, waiting for requests from Gopher clients. Historically, Gopher has been used to automate searches for specific information on the Internet. Its popularity is on the decline, as Web-based search engines are quickly replacing Gopher as the searching tools of choice on the Internet.

Telnet

5 Prior to the emergence of the Web, *Telnet* was the primary means of getting around on the Internet. This UNIX-based system is fast and reliable. However, it is purely text-based and often requires *shell* programs, which activate complex UNIX functions through simple menu-driven user commands, making it easier to use.

What Is the Web?

The World Wide Web (WWW, W3, or the Web for short) is the most visual part of the Internet. It is also the fastest growing part of the Internet, which may be because it is so easy to access and explore. It is based on the display of *Web pages*, which are computer documents that can present text, graphics, and sounds. A Web page represents a single location on the Web. When you are "on the Web" you can usually only see one Web page at a time. A Web *site* is made up of two or more interconnected Web pages presented as a unified place on the Web. Some sites have a handful of pages; a few have hundreds.

1 The Web is visual, allowing you to see more than just text on your computer screen. For example, with the Web you can preview a piece of art and then download it, copying it to your own computer.

TIP SHEET

▶ **A common term used on the Web is *home page*. This is the intended central or starting place on a Web site. It is usually the first page of that a visitor sees and is often used as a guide for exploring the rest of the Web site.**

▶ **There is no standard definition of a Web site, and the extent of each site is left entirely up to the designer. In practical terms, however, a Web site usually refers to a grouping of interconnected pages that have a common thematic and graphical structure.**

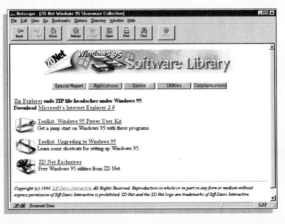

5 Web pages also serve as an ideal medium for transferring computer software. Many corporate Web sites, for example, allow users to download free demonstration programs, add-on pieces, or upgrades to existing computer applications.

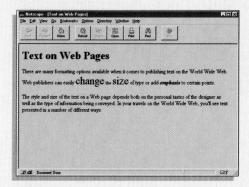

2 You can still view written information as well, but text can be formatted in different ways to fit the overall presentation of the Web page.

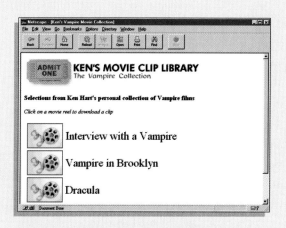

3 The Web is an ideal medium for the transmission of multimedia information. With the click of a button you can download a clip from your favorite movie or hear a snippet of audio from a famous radio address.

4 The Web's highly graphical nature makes it ideal for presenting artwork and photographic images. Pictures of family, friends, and especially pets have become increasingly popular among Web page creators.

How Does the Web Function?

The Web's visual appeal is very compelling. However, the Web's popularity is also based on its inherent ability to transport the user to other Web pages and even to other parts of the Internet. This massive connectivity forms the fundamental core of the World Wide Web. All these connections are easily made with the click of a mouse button using a process called *linking*. Through a common computer language called Hypertext Markup Language (HTML), images, words, or anything else on a Web page can become a link. Web links are also commonly known as hyperlinks.

1 HTML and hyperlinks are the basis of the Web's versatility. Links on a Web page can take the viewer to another place on the same Web page or to a different Web page altogether. They can be links to images, or they can activate the transfer of digitized information such as video or audio clips. Hyperlinks can call up a window for sending e-mail, or even take the viewer to locations on the Internet outside of the Web.

TIP SHEET

▶ **One way to understand hypertext is to think of it as a metaphor for the way the human mind works. Inside the brain, ideas lead to other ideas, and thoughts connect to other thoughts in random, unstructured patterns. Hypertext allows for the same freedom of movement between interrelated or even unrelated concepts and ideas.**

▶ **On the Web, a hyperlink on one Web page can connect to another Web page on the same computer, or it can connect to a Web site on a computer on the other side of the planet.**

4 Web pages usually have several hyperlinks, sometimes even hundreds. Because the choice is entirely up to the viewer as to which of these hyperlinks to follow, there is no way to predict the path that users may follow as they explore the Web.

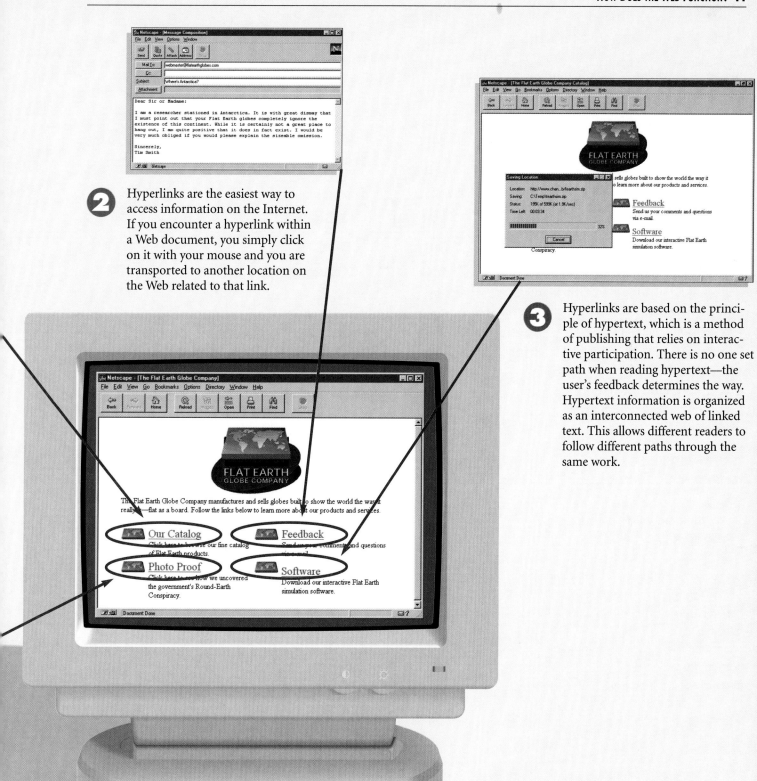

2 Hyperlinks are the easiest way to access information on the Internet. If you encounter a hyperlink within a Web document, you simply click on it with your mouse and you are transported to another location on the Web related to that link.

3 Hyperlinks are based on the principle of hypertext, which is a method of publishing that relies on interactive participation. There is no one set path when reading hypertext—the user's feedback determines the way. Hypertext information is organized as an interconnected web of linked text. This allows different readers to follow different paths through the same work.

What Can You Do on the Web?

The World Wide Web offers a countless number of resources that appeal to all types of users. The Web is a growing community, and most Web site creators soon find that the best way to get people to visit their sites is to offer interactivity and create a compelling reason for visitors to return. A few of the primary ways people interact on the Web are presented here.

1 One of the original purposes for the development of the Web and the Internet as a whole was to be a tool to support research. College, university, government, and private industry sites offer a wealth of information on just about any topic.

TIP SHEET

▶ Web users who do not have their own Web page can still contribute to the general welfare of the whole Web community by taking part in surveys and interactive demonstrations offered by Web site developers. Feedback from Web users help Web developers find out what the public wants and how to deliver it.

▶ Original and fresh ideas are being incorporated on the World Wide Web all the time. One of the best places on the Web to go if you want to keep up with what's new is the Cool Site of the Day. To visit, point your Web browser to http://cool.infi.net. You'll learn more about using your Web browser in the next few chapters.

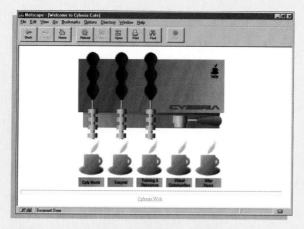

2 With so many millions of people on the Web, sites targeted to special interests can find a niche among like-minded individuals with an ease that was never possible before the development of the Internet and the Web. You can use the Web to find people who share your ideas, hobbies, and pastimes.

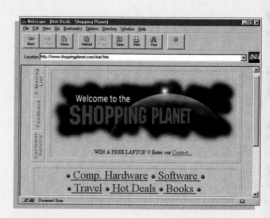

3 On the Web, shoppers will find a whole new world of possibilities. Detailed product descriptions, complete with full-color photos, give shoppers an easy way to find the goods and services they desire without leaving their own home.

4 With many companies building sites on the Web, you can access an entire range of services. The Web can become a marketing cornerstone for companies that want to provide easily accessible customer follow-up and support. Many computer software developers have already created vast Web sites with just this goal in mind. New software updates and add-ons can be offered to customers with very little expense.

What Else Can You Do on the Web?

The list of possibilities goes on and on. Here are a few more popular uses for the Web. You'll learn how to find Web sites devoted to specific interests in later chapters.

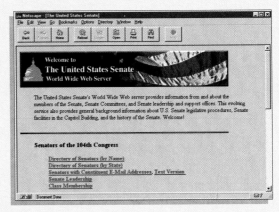

▶ **1** The U.S. government operates a large number of Web sites. The Web is ideal for learning more about the government, and for contacting your representatives and officials. If you want to track a bill before Congress, send a message to the President, or find out more about your local and state governments, the Web is a great place to start.

TIP SHEET

▶ Information on using search engines and navigational aids is explored further in Chapter 7.

▶ Thanks to NASA and the National Weather Service, it is now possible to get detailed weather maps, track storms, and determine if you should wash your car based on direct satellite feeds from space. The URL for the National Weather Service is http://www.nws.noaa.gov/.

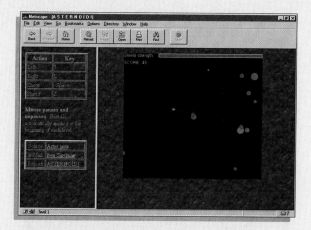

2 Who says the Web has to be all work and no play? Certainly not the people who have concocted Web sites for every game and social activity imaginable. Everything from interactive card games to tips and hints on how to find the hidden treasure with your favorite CD-ROM game is available on the Web.

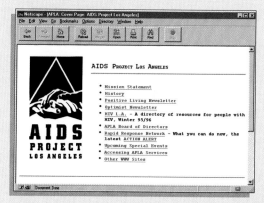

3 The Web is also a great way to meet other concerned individuals and get up-to-the-minute information on a variety of social ills and health concerns. AIDS awareness and support groups, for instance, have used the Web extensively, as have drug and alcohol treatment programs.

4 Of course, the Web and the Internet are famous for offering up-to-date news and statistical information, such as current weather conditions, business or commercial trends and market reports, the latest headlines, and information in a variety of fields such as politics, the arts, media and entertainment, science, education, and much more.

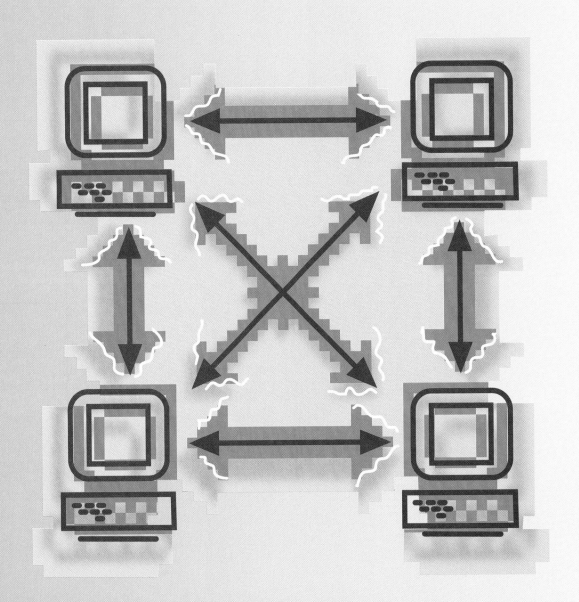

CHAPTER 2

How to Connect to the Web

To access the Web you typically need three things: a computer, Internet access, and the proper software to make it all work.

This chapter assumes that you already own a personal computer running Windows 3.1 or Windows 95. If you're connecting to the Web from home or a small office, it's likely that you'll need a modem as well. The graphical nature of the Web demands a high-speed connection, and modem speed is measured in bits transferred per second, commonly abbreviated as *bps*. We'll talk more about modem speed on the next few pages.

For service providers, the power of the marketplace continues to drive down the price of Web access. More and more providers enter the market each day, and most of them now have Web access.

The best part is that most of the software you'll need is free and easy to use. If you're running Windows 95 with the Microsoft Plus! pack, you already have all the software you need to make your first Internet connection. Once you're online, you'll be able to get the latest software updates and new releases for taking full advantage of the World Wide Web.

Getting Started

This section is an overview of what you'll need to connect to the Internet and World Wide Web. You probably already have at least two of these things—a computer and telephone service. If so, you're already halfway there. The rest is easy.

▶ **1** Let's start with hardware—your computer. It would be hard to find a computer these days that wouldn't be able to connect to the Web, especially since the minimum requirement for a PC is that you are able to run Microsoft Windows or the IBM OS/2 operating system. This means having a 386 processor or better.

TIP SHEET

▸ **Many modems ship with communications software. Some also come with disks or coupons for signing up with a major online service such as AOL. Look for these extra bonuses when you choose your modem.**

▸ **Before you begin surfing the Web extensively, you'll want to make sure that you have at least 8 megabytes of RAM and 25 megabytes of free hard-disk space. You'll get the best results with a Pentium or 486 microprocessor.**

5 Finally, you will need the proper software. In most cases, all the software you need, as well as instructions for setting it up, will be provided by your ISP. Later in this chapter, you will learn everything you need to know about configuring versions of the most popular Internet access software for the PC.

2 You also need a modem. A 9,600 bps modem is the base requirement for connecting to the Internet, but for graphical Web access, you will want a modem that can handle at least 14,400 bps. The preferred speed for a modem is 28,800 bps or above.

3 Next, you need an Internet Service Provider (ISP). ISPs serve as your gateway to the Internet. There are many different types of ISPs, and they offer a wide range of services. You might choose to work with a local ISP or use one of the larger commercial online services, such as America Online (AOL) or CompuServe.

4 Each ISP has its own specific requirements and limitations for Internet access. It's always a good idea to choose an ISP with a proven customer service record. You may need to talk directly with a representative to configure your system for Internet access. You'll learn even more about what to look for in an ISP later in this chapter.

How to Choose a Modem

A modem is the piece of equipment that links you to the Internet through your phone line. The modem's primary function is to translate information coming over the phone lines into a format that your computer can process.

▶ **1** There are many types of modems to choose from, and they are available in a number of styles. Some modems are external, and attach to your computer via a special modem cable. Other modems are internal and plug directly into one of your computer's peripheral slots. Either type will work fine. Even the simplest and least expensive modems will do just about everything you need.

6 New technologies such as Integrated Services Digital Network (ISDN) and cable modems are beginning to become available. These types of connections offer incredibly fast access to the Web, and will most likely replace today's modems once the connections and required hardware become widely available.

TIP SHEET

▶ If you are having trouble getting the maximum performance out your 28,800 bps modem, many add-on cards are available that can help bypass transmission bottlenecks you may encounter. Add-on cards are available at most computer stores.

▶ Internal modems leave the factory with standard jumper and serial port settings. Consult your manual to ensure that these settings are correct for your type of computer.

2 The first thing you should look for in a modem is its speed. Modem speed is measured in terms of how much data it can process in one second. This data is measured in bits.

3 Make sure you choose a modem that is capable of transfer rates of 14,400 bits per second (bps) or faster. You can use a slower modem to connect to the Internet and even to access much of the Web, but you probably wouldn't enjoy the experience. Many Web pages can be very slow to load, especially if they feature a large amount of graphics. With a low-speed modem connection, it can take several minutes to load each Web page. It is strongly recommended that you invest in a 28,000 bps modem. The difference in speed is very noticeable.

4 You should also look for a modem that has additional features such as data compression, which allows the modem to squeeze more data through the phone line than the actual transmission speed indicates. A 14,400 bps modem with compression can push through files at rates up to 19,200 bps. The newer high-speed modems also tend to feature built-in error-checking that helps reduce problems associated with phone line noise and other transmission problems.

5 Faster modems rated at 28,800 bps (also called V.34, V.Fast, or V.FC) are available at very low prices, most costing less than $200. The faster 28,800 bps modems are quickly becoming the standard for Web access.

How to Choose a Local Internet Service Provider

The World Wide Web has been called the Gold Rush of the 1990s. If that's true, then Internet Service Providers are the ones who sell the picks and shovels. There are many important factors to consider when choosing your Internet Service Provider (ISP). Cost, ease of access, customer service, and reliability all need to be considered. Fortunately, with the incredible popularity of the Web, there are a large number of ISPs to choose from. If you do some careful shopping, you'll be able to find an ISP that meets your needs perfectly. In this section, you'll learn what to look for and what to avoid when deciding on an ISP.

▶ **1** Make sure your prospective ISP can offer what you need. To access the Web, you need either a SLIP (Serial Line Internet Protocol) or PPP (Point-to-Point Protocol) connection. These special types of connections are different than a simple dial-up Internet connection. Make sure your ISP knows that you require access to the World Wide Web.

TIP SHEET

▶ **You may want to inquire about the ISP's own connection to the Internet. Since the Net is a network of networks, your ISP needs a fast connection to the Internet to provide the best service. Ask your ISP for a diagram or explanation of how they connect to other networks and at what speeds.**

▶ **Some ISPs bundle services and offer different access packages. Ask about all the pricing and access plans they offer so that you don't end up paying for options you don't need or want.**

6 Choosing the right ISP involves asking some basic questions that require basic answers. You don't need to get into a lot of technical jargon to know if a prospective ISP will be able to provide the level of service you need. The illustration here shows some good questions to ask.

2 Another key factor in choosing an ISP is locality. Ideally, your ISP should be based in your local calling area, to eliminate the need to make long-distance phone calls. An alternative is to select a commercial online service or larger nationwide ISP, both of which tend to provide local dial-in numbers to their networks.

3 Access speed is an important factor. Make sure your ISP can support the use of high-speed modems. Even if you have a fast 28,800 bps modem on your computer, it won't do you much good if your ISP only has a 14,400 bps modem on its end.

4 Service and support are very important parts of choosing an ISP. Your ISP should be willing to make it easy for you to get online, walking you through the setup process if necessary. You should also look for an ISP that provides free and immediate technical support in case you run into problems with your connection down the road.

5 If you plan on creating your own home page on the Web someday, you may want to ask your prospective ISP if they offer space on their system to host your Web pages. Keep in mind, however, that you don't need to use the same ISP for both dial-up access and Web page hosting. You can shop around for the best rates for each type of service. You'll learn more about creating your own home page on the Web in Chapter 12.

Internet Service Provider Checklist

☑ Does the ISP have 24-hour service, 7 days a week? Do they have tech people on site 24 hours a day, or are they just on call?

☑ Do they have backup equipment? What happens if their gear breaks down?

☑ Do they continually monitor the network? Or do you have to call them when there is trouble?

☑ Do they have an 800 phone line for trouble calls? If you are out of the dialing area and still need help, who pays for the long-distance phone call?

☑ Do they have adequate staff on their support lines, or do you have to wait on hold for a long period of time?

☑ Do they focus on Web service alone, or do they also provide other kinds of access for customers? If the latter is true, do they have a dedicated server just for Web clients?

How to Configure Your Windows 95 Internet Software

Windows 95 is designed to be ready to connect to the Internet with ease. To do this, you'll need a copy of the Windows 95 Plus! Pack, which is available separately. Some new computers come with the Internet portion of the Plus! pack already installed; check with your computer manufacturer to see if this applies to you.

Once you have the necessary components, it's as simple as following the instructions of a Setup Wizard. You'll need some basic information from your ISP before you begin, however. Despite the ease of setting up the Windows 95 Internet software, you may want to have your ISP on the phone while you set it up to help answer any questions you might have.

TIP SHEET

▶ You can create a shortcut to your ISP by dragging the icon from the Dial-Up Networking folder to your desktop. This can be especially helpful if you have more than one ISP and like to switch between accounts.

▶ To change information about your ISP, such as the phone number or IP address, right-click on the icon for your ISP and choose Properties from the context menu. You can change all the information you entered about your ISP in this section.

1 Double-click on the Internet icon on your Windows 95 desktop. If there is no Internet icon on the desktop, you'll need to install the Microsoft Plus! pack before proceeding. When you click on the icon, one of two things will happen. If you're already set up for Internet access, your Web browser will launch and you can skip this section. If you are not already set up for access, the Internet Setup Wizard window will appear. Click on the Next button to proceed.

10 You're now ready to connect to the Internet. You can dial your ISP at any time either by double-clicking on the Internet icon on the desktop or by choosing a specific ISP from the Dial-Up Networking folder, which is accessible from the Accessories folder on your Start menu.

9 If your ISP also gave you an Internet e-mail account, enter your e-mail information in this screen. If you do not plan to use Internet Mail, uncheck the box. When you're finished, press the Next button. If you decided to use Exchange for your e-mail, you'll be prompted to choose an Exchange profile setting. When you're finished entering all the information, press Next button.

8 Enter your Domain Name Server (DNS) address, along with an alternate address, if available. You should obtain these numbers from your ISP. Press the Next button when you're finished.

2 If you plan to use the Microsoft Network as your Internet Service Provider, select Use the Microsoft Network. If you have a different ISP, select that option. Press the Next button when you're finished.

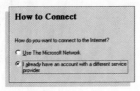

3 The next screen will prompt you about using Microsoft Exchange to send and receive Internet Mail. Make your choice here and press the Next button. If you choose to use Exchange, the Setup Wizard will install the necessary software. For more information on Microsoft Exchange, refer to your Windows 95 documentation.

4 The Setup Wizard will then prompt you to begin entering some information about your Internet Service Provider. Type in the name of your ISP in the text box. Then press the Next button to continue.

5 Type in the area code and phone number to connect to your ISP. If your ISP requires you to perform special commands on their system prior to establishing your Internet access, check the box that enables a terminal window after dialing. Check with your ISP beforehand to see if this is necessary. Press the Next button when you're finished.

6 Type in your user name and password in the text boxes. The user name and password are assigned to you by your ISP and should be typed in exactly as they appear on whatever documentation your ISP provided. Press the Next button to move onto the next step.

7 The next screen concerns IP address information. If your Internet Service Provider's system automatically assigns you an IP address each time you connect, choose the first option. If you use the same IP address each time, choose the second option and enter the IP address and Subnet Mask numbers. You'll need to obtain those numbers from your ISP. Press the Next button to continue.

How to Configure Your Windows 3.1 Internet Software

Most service providers give you all the software you need to get started for free. Using simple communications applications that come bundled with nearly all commercial modems, you can usually get online with a provider, sign up for an account, and download all the software you need for full Web access. For Web access you will need an account and some software. The kind of account you'll need is called an IP, or *Internet Protocol* account, and the essential piece of software for accessing the Web with a PC is called a TCP/IP stack. One popular version for Windows 3.1 is Trumpet Winsock, a shareware application from Trumpet Software.

This section assumes that you are familiar with the Windows 3.1 Program Manager and File Manager. It also assumes that you are comfortable with modifying your AUTOEXEC.BAT system file. If you're not familiar with these operations, you should seek help when installing your software.

TIP SHEET

▶ **IP accounts come in two types: SLIP (Serial Line Internet Protocol) and PPP (Point-to-Point Protocol). Both do basically the same thing, but PPP tends to be more stable and produces better results. If you have a choice, choose PPP.**

▶ **Trumpet Winsock uses a login.cmd file created with a text editor for entering phone numbers and other essential information your provider requires. Most providers will either send you a preformatted login.cmd file or instructions for properly configuring and placing this file on your hard drive.**

▶ **①** Often, Trumpet Winsock or some other TCP/IP stack will come bundled in a "Starter Kit" from your ISP. You may need to download the software from your ISP or have them send you a copy on disk. Make sure you contact your ISP and ask any questions you might have about obtaining the necessary software.

⑦ If all goes well you should see a connection established, and Trumpet will tell you your IP address. If things don't seem to be working, go back to the setup.cmd command on the Dialler menu and make sure you used the right username and password. Many connection problems are simply due to errors in usernames or passwords.

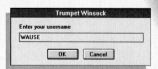

⑥ The first time you log in with Trumpet it will ask you for your username and password. Make sure to  enter the IP password and not your UNIX (dial-up) password if you have one. This is the only place you enter your IP password. When you log in after this, you will only have to select Login from the Dialler menu. You will not have to enter the username and password each time. Trumpet Winsock stores these in its memory.

2 Create a new directory on your hard drive, such as C:\TRUMPET, and place the Trumpet Winsock software in that directory. You should also create a Program Manager group for your Internet software, and create an icon for the TCPMAN.EXE file. It's also a good idea to add C:\TRUMPET to the PATH statement in your AUTOEXEC.BAT file.

3 Double-click on the Trumpet Winsock icon you just created. Since you are running TCPMAN.EXE for the first time, you will see the Network Configuration window. If for some reason this window does not immediately appear, choose Setup from the File menu.

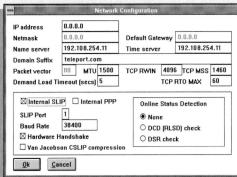

4 Many ISPs will preset the necessary configuration options for you. If not, you'll need to obtain the correct settings directly from your ISP. Specifically, you'll need the following information: your provider's Name and Time Server, your provider's Domain Suffix, your account type (SLIP or PPP), your SLIP Port, and your Baud Rate (which depends on your modem type and speed). If you're not already familiar with these settings, it is a good idea to have your ISP walk you through the setup process.

5 Click OK and exit Trumpet. You must exit for the settings to take effect. Double-click on the Trumpet Winsock icon again and choose Login from the Dialler menu.

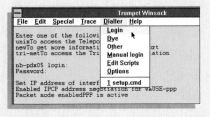

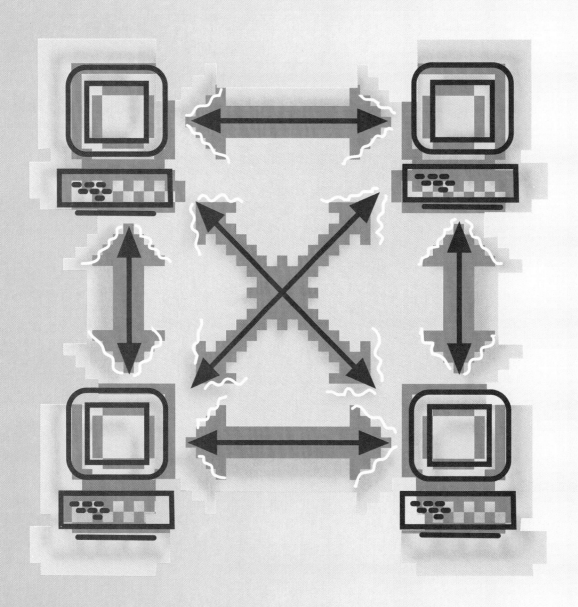

CHAPTER 3

Web Navigation 101

 Web browsers are programs used to explore the Web. A Web browser's main functions are to interpret hypertext documents, read URLs, and navigate the Web's intricate structure of hyperlinks.

Many browsers use color, icons, pull-down menus, and buttons to make Web exploration easy and fun. They also remember where you have been and can store markers, making it easy to go back to places you want to revisit.

There are two basic kinds of browsers: text-only browsers and graphical browsers. Text-only browsers (also called line-mode browsers) don't display graphics. They were the original Web browsers, developed by no-nonsense Web users who were primarily interested in using the Web as a research tool.

With the Web's maturation into a full-fledged publishing medium, graphical browsers have become the norm. Besides being pretty to look at, graphical browsers are more interactive, easier to navigate the Web with, and can also take advantage of greater presentation and layout controls. In this chapter, we'll take a look at how Web browers help you explore the Web.

How Browsers Work

Browsers interpret documents created with hypertext programming and display them in a user-friendly format, commonly known as the Web page. There are many different browsers used by people to explore the Web, and each one has its advantages and disadvantages. But the primary function they must all fulfill is to make it possible for the user to navigate the Web.

▶ **1** All browsers work with a TCP/IP connection either through a dial-up SLIP or PPP account, or through a direct line. If you're lucky enough to have a direct connection to the Internet, you'll have much faster access to the Web.

TIP SHEET

▸ **Many browsers are freeware or shareware, and some come bundled in pre-packaged "Internet Kits" like Spry's Internet in a Box or Netcom's Netcruiser.**

▸ **There are many different Web browsers to choose from. If you don't like the way your Web browser operates, it's possible that another browser will fit your style. A good place to find all of the freely available Web browsers is at the Yahoo! Site. The URL is http://www.yahoo.com/Computers _and_Internet/Internet/World_Wide _Web/Browsers/.**

5 Most browsers show hyperlinks as highlighted text that is underlined and displayed in some color other than normal text. Graphical browsers take advantage of your computer's mouse, letting you simply point and click on any hyperlink that looks interesting. Line-mode browsers generally don't use a mouse, and they force the user to use the keyboard to navigate hyperlinks.

2 Some browsers can only display the text shown on Web pages, others can display Web pages with full color graphics. Most graphical browsers include an option to turn off the graphical display for faster loading of Web pages.

3 Browsers let you control your own pathway through the Internet and the Web. You don't have to rely on other people's hyperlinks to take you where you want to go. Instead, you can just type in the desired address (URL), and your browser will look for that location on the Web.

Make any page on the Web your starting point.

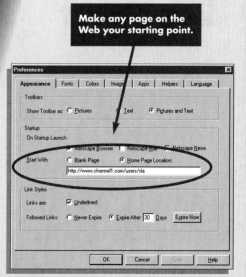

4 Most browsers go to a prescribed location (default) when you first open them. You can change this setting to automatically find your favorite starting point each time you launch your Web browser.

How to Read a Web Address

Almost every item of information on the World Wide Web can be accessed directly. That's because every document, file, and image has its own specific address. These addresses are called Uniform Resource Locators (URLs). URLs are used by Web browsing software to locate and access information on the World Wide Web. It's sometimes easy to understand if you think of URLs as postal addresses for the Internet.

TIP SHEET

▶ Be very careful when typing in the URL. The Web is very unforgiving with URLs, and will only accept exact matches. If you receive a "document not found" message when trying to access a page on the Web, check to see if the URL has been typed in correctly.

Location: http://www.zdnet.com/~zdi/software/win95/utils.html#WINZIP

1 The first part of the URL is known as the protocol. This is almost always http://, which is short for Hypertext Transfer Protocol. Some URLs will start with different protocols, such as ftp:// and news://. If you're accessing a document on your local machine instead of on the Web, the URL will begin with file://.

Location: http://www.zdnet.com/~zdi/software/win95/utils.html#WINZIP

2 The second part of the URL is known as the domain name. If you've used e-mail on the Internet, you're probably already familiar with domains. The domain represents the name of the server that you're connecting to.

press.com

Location: http://www.zdnet.com/~zdi/software/win95/utils.html#WINZIP

3 The third part of the URL is called the directory path. This is the specific area on the server where the item resides. Directory paths on Web servers work a lot like they do on your desktop computer.

Location: http://www.zdnet.com/~zdi/software/win95/utils.html#WINZIP

4 The fourth part of the URL is called the document file name. This points to the specific file being accessed. This is usually an HTML file, but it can also be an image, sound, or another file.

Location: http://www.zdnet.com/~zdi/software/win95/utils.html#WINZIP

5 Sometimes, the URL contains a fifth part, known as the anchor name. This is a pointer to a specific part of an HTML document. It's always preceded by a pound sign. Anchors are especially useful for large documents.

Understanding File Transfer on the Web

One of the most common activities on the Web is downloading software. Most downloading is performed using FTP (File Transfer Protocol), which technically is separate from the World Wide Web. But accessing FTP sites and downloading software with a Web browser is such a seamless process that you may never know you've left the Web at all. There are many ways to find and download software from FTP sites with your Web browser. One of the best sites is clnet's shareware.com, a popular starting point on the Web for finding downloadable software.

TIP SHEET

► It helps to be as specific as possible when searching for a particular piece of software. Searching by generic terms can yield hundreds or even thousands of results. Once you become familiar with basic searching on the Web, you may want to try using some of the "power search" engines that are available on clnet and other sites.

► Most software on the Web is compressed in ZIP format. WinZip, the program we downloaded in this example, is ideal for uncompressing ZIP archives. You can search for WinZip yourself, or download it directly from the WinZip home page at http://www.winzip.com.

❶ Using your Web browser, jump to the home page for clnet's shareware.com site by typing **http://www.shareware.com/** in the URL entry box of your browser. This entry box should be prominently displayed right under the menu bar in your browser menu. You'll learn more about using some of the most popular Web browsers in Chapter 4.

❾ Once you've selected a file name and location, your Web browser will initiate the FTP transfer. The file will be copied from the remote system to your local computer. The total time of the transfer depends on the size of the file and the speed of your Internet connection. Most Web browsers feature a status bar to give you an indication of how much time is left in the transfer.

❽ After your browser successfully connects, it will prompt you for a file name and location for the file that will be copied to your system. Enter a file name and click on the Save button when you're finished.

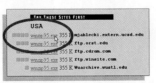

❼ Select a site to download from by clicking on the corresponding hyperlink. Generally, you'll have the most success with sites near your geographic location that have high ratings. If your browser has trouble connecting to the site, choose one of the alternates instead.

❻ The next screen that appears is the download options screen. On this screen, clnet presents all of the known FTP locations for the file you want to download. A rating guide helps you determine the best connection, based on download speed and location.

2 Place the cursor over the word Search and click the mouse button. This action triggers a hyperlink that takes you to cInet's search page.

3 A search form asks you a few important questions about what type of software you're looking for. In this example, we'll assume that we're looking for a program called WinZip, which is a popular utility for working with ZIP archive files. If you're not already familiar with ZIP files, you soon will be. ZIP files are very common on the Internet.

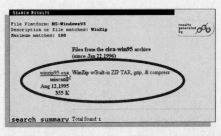

4 To begin the search, you need to fill in the important information about your search criteria. In the Select Platform box, choose MS-Windows95. In the first search word box, type **WinZip**. You can leave the other fields as they are for now. When you're finished, click on the Start Search button.

5 After a few moments, a new page will appear in your Web browser window with the results of the search. In this example, one result was returned, and it's exactly the program we were looking for. Click on the hyperlink marked winzip95.exe to continue.

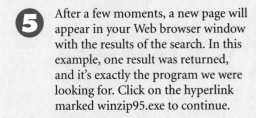

CHAPTER 4

Web Surfing with Netscape, NCSA Mosaic, and Internet Explorer

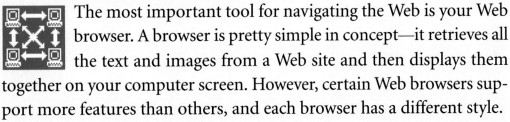 The most important tool for navigating the Web is your Web browser. A browser is pretty simple in concept—it retrieves all the text and images from a Web site and then displays them together on your computer screen. However, certain Web browsers support more features than others, and each browser has a different style.

From a crowded field of available Web browsers, three have emerged as favorites: Netscape Navigator, NCSA Mosaic, and Microsoft Internet Explorer. Of the three, Netscape is clearly the most popular and is also the most technically advanced.

In this chapter, you'll get an introduction to the "Big Three" and take a quick peek at some of the most important features that each browser has to offer. You'll also revisit some of the Web browsing basics that were covered in the previous chapter. Keep in mind that although these three browsers are the most popular, there are plenty of other choices available, and you're certain to find a Web browser that fits your tastes. Finding the perfect browser isn't always an easy task, but this quick tour might help you choose one over the other.

How to Browse the Web with Netscape Navigator

Netscape Navigator, known to many simply as Netscape, is the most popular browser in use today. In fact, many sources estimate that 70–80 percent of everyone browsing the Web is using Netscape.

One of the reasons for Netscape's incredible popularity is its extensive support for new features. The programmers at Netscape Communications constantly update their work, and push the envelope of Web technology with each new release. In this section, we'll take a close look at how you can navigate the Web with Netscape.

 1 Netscape is available for many different platforms, including Windows 95, Windows 3.1, Macintosh, and UNIX. You can download the latest evaluation versions of the program by visiting the Netscape download page at http://home.netscape.com/comprod/mirror/index.html. You can also download them directly via FTP at ftp1.netscape.com.

 7 You can access Netscape's bookmark management features by pressing Ctrl+B or selecting Go To Bookmarks from the Bookmarks menu option. Netscape allows you to sort your bookmarks, arrange groups of them in folders, and edit the properties for each item. You can even have Netscape automatically check all of the bookmarked sites to see if the pages have been updated since the last time you visited—just select What's New? from the File menu.

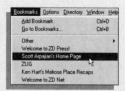

 6 Netscape remembers your favorite Web pages by using bookmarks. If you want to create a permanent link to the current page, press Ctrl+D to create a bookmark. You can instantly jump to any of your marked pages by selecting it from the Bookmarks menu.

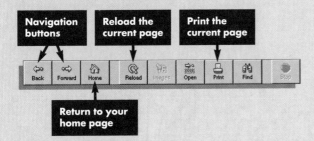

Navigation buttons

Reload the current page

Print the current page

Return to your home page

2 Netscape features a simple toolbar for navigating the Web, including buttons to move backward and forward through pages you've visited, as well as a button to reload the current page. Several other options, including printing and searching, are also available from the toolbar.

3 You can jump immediately to any site on the Web by typing its URL in the Location box and pressing Enter. You can also click on the Open button from the toolbar to achieve the same result. If you click on the small arrow at the right of the Location box, you'll see a list of URLs for Web pages that you recently visited.

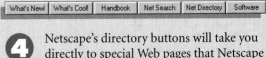

4 Netscape's directory buttons will take you directly to special Web pages that Netscape Communications maintains. These pages keep you up to date on what's new and cool on the Web. You can also use the Search button to find just about any Web site that is available.

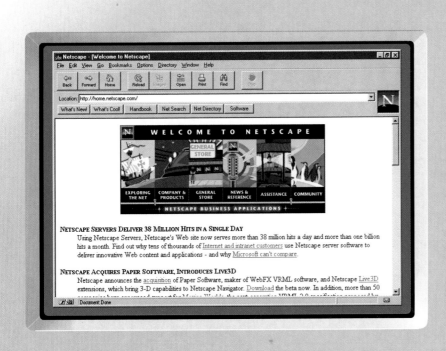

5 Hyperlinks allow you to jump to another page on the Web. Normally, hyperlink text is underlined and appears in a different color on the Web page. Netscape gives you an additional visual clue as well—when the mouse cursor passes over a hyperlink, it changes to a hand with a pointing finger.

How to Browse the Web with Netscape Navigator (Continued)

▶⑧ Netscape 2.0 supports context-sensitive menus. If you right-click your mouse in the browser window, you'll have quick access to special features.

TIP SHEET

▶ **Many of the features covered in this section require Netscape Navigator 2.0. If you're not using the latest version of this popular Web browser, be sure to download it by visiting Netscape's home page.**

▶ **You can learn even more about Netscape Navigator by reading *How to Use Netscape Navigator 2.0* by Rich Schwerin (Ziff-Davis Press).**

⑬ Netscape 2.0 also supports the use of plug-ins to view different types of file formats inside the browser window. Each plug-in is designed to view a single type of file. For example, the Adobe Acrobat plug-in allows you to view Acrobat (.PDF) files. A complete list of plug-ins available for Netscape 2.0 is available at http://home.netscape.com/assist/helper_apps/variety.html.

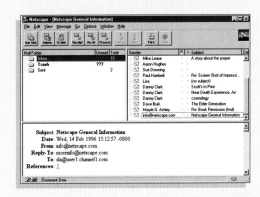

 Netscape Navigator 2.0 adds e-mail capabilities to the browser. Now you can read and reply to e-mail messages in a separate window. To access Netscape's e-mail features, choose Netscape Mail from the Window menu.

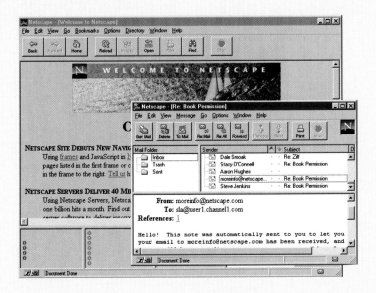

10 You can also maintain an address book of e-mail contacts. Netscape allows you to assign nicknames to your e-mail addresses and store multiple names in groups to save typing. You can access the address book from the Window menu.

11 Netscape 2.0 also includes a built-in Usenet newsgroup reader. You can browse, read, and post messages to any newsgroup as long as you have access to a news server. Choose Netscape News from the Window menu to access the reader.

12 Netscape 2.0 supports the Java programming language, which allows Web designers to incorporate small applications, commonly called "applets," into their Web sites. Java applets can be used to accomplish a number of things previously impossible on the Web, including real-time games and stock quote tickers. The applets work right inside your Netscape browser window, so there's nothing you need to add or do to experience Java with Netscape.

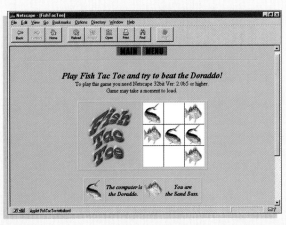

How to Browse the Web with NCSA Mosaic

NCSA Mosaic was the first graphical browser to hit the Web. Developed by the National Center for Supercomputing Applications at the University of Illinois at Urbana-Champaign, Mosaic was a ground-breaking application and is largely responsible for the immense popularity of the Web.

While Netscape's developers have been adding bells and whistles to their browser at an incredible pace, the programmers of NCSA Mosaic have largely stuck to the existing HTML standards. This means that NCSA Mosaic doesn't support all of the HTML extensions. However, NCSA Mosaic is still one of the best overall browsers and includes a few innovations of its own.

 NCSA Mosaic is available for several different platforms, including Windows 95 and Windows 3.1. However, Windows 3.1 users will need to install the optional Win32s libraries before using Mosaic. NCSA Mosaic is free, and the latest version can be downloaded from the NCSA home page at http://www.ncsa.uiuc.edu.

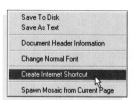

 NCSA Mosaic supports context-sensitive menus. If you right-click your mouse in the browser window, you'll have quick access to special features.

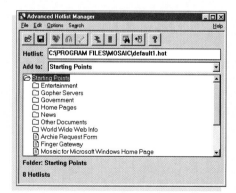

 You can edit and maintain your Hotlist using the Advanced Hotlist Manager, which is accessible from the Navigate menu. The Advanced Hotlist Manager allows you to add, edit, and delete URLs, as well as organize them in folders. NCSA Mosaic comes packaged with a Hotlist already filled with interesting and popular sites on the Web.

Navigation buttons   **Return to your home page**

Reload the current page

2 NCSA Mosaic's toolbar allows you to access most of the program's key features. You can browse through Web pages you've already visited using the forward and backward navigation buttons. The "home" button instantly takes you back to your predefined home page on the Web. The toolbar also contains buttons for other common activities, such as printing, searching, and cut and paste functions.

3 You can jump immediately to any site on the Web by typing in the URL in the Location bar and pressing Enter or clicking on the green check box. You can also click on the Open Folder button from the toolbar or select Open Document from the File Menu. NCSA Mosaic maintains a short history of Web pages you recently visited, which is accessible by clicking on the small arrow at the right of the Location bar.

This is a Hyperlink.

4 Hyperlinks allow you to jump to another page on the Web. NCSA Mosaic normally displays hyperlink text in a different color than the normal text on the page. When the mouse cursor passes over a hyperlink, it changes to a hand with a pointing finger.

5 NCSA Mosaic allows you to store your favorite Web pages in special Hotlists. You can add the current page to your Hotlist by typing the letter A on the keyboard, or by choosing the Add Current to Hotlist option from the Navigate menu. To jump immediately to any page in your Hotlist, simply select it from the Hotlist menu.

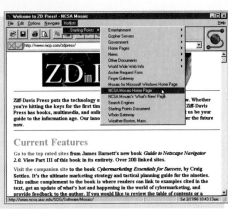

How to Browse the Web with NCSA Mosaic (Continued)

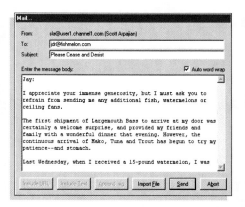

▶ **8** You can send e-mail directly from NCSA Mosaic by choosing Send E-mail from the File menu. You can include the URL and text from the current Web page in your message, as well as import a file from your local system. One significant limitation of the e-mail capabilities in NCSA Mosaic is that you can only send messages to one recipient at a time.

TIP SHEET

▶ **You can use NCSA Mosaic's Collaborate feature to take friends on a tour of your favorite sites. To set up a Web Tour, initiate a Collaborative session with you as the host, and then wait for your fellow NCSA Mosaic users to join the same session.**

▶ **NCSA Mosaic's AutoSurf feature is ideal for reading an online publication such as a daily newspaper. You can have NCSA Mosaic retrieve the front page and one or two levels of pages below it. Then, you can read through the daily news at your leisure, while you're disconnected from the Internet.**

 You can control the AutoSurf session by changing the settings in the Setup window. AutoSurf will follow all the links on the starting page and pages below it up to the maximum level you specify. You can also limit your AutoSurf session to a single Web server and specify a maximum number of pages to retrieve. Additional options allow you to choose whether to load images and display the Web pages as they are read.

9 NCSA Mosaic allows you to read Usenet newsgroups. You must have an Internet Provider that operates a newsgroup server running the NNTP news protocol. To access the newsgroups, choose Newsgroups from the File menu.

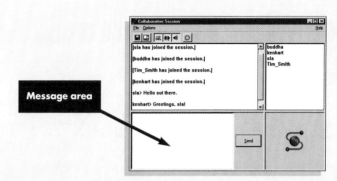

Message area

10 The Collaborate feature of NCSA Mosaic allows you to participate in joint sessions with fellow Web surfers. You can link your Mosaic session with other Mosaic users, chat, and exchange files and data. The Collaborate feature is a client-server system, which means that one user acts as the server, or host. The other participants in the session act as clients, or guests. To access the Collaborate feature, choose Collaborate from the File menu.

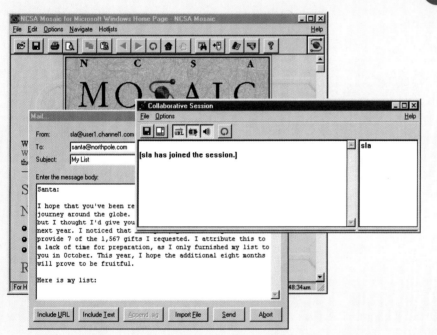

11 Like most Web browsers, NCSA Mosaic uses a disk cache to store recently visited Web pages on your local system. For most people, reading a page from a disk cache is significantly faster than reading it over the Internet. NCSA Mosaic's AutoSurf allows you to automatically retrieve pages and store them in your disk cache. In addition to saving time, this feature can save you money if you pay substantial connect-time charges to access the Internet. To use AutoSurf, choose Mosaic AutoSurf from the Navigate menu.

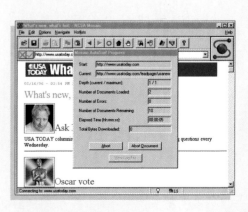

How to Browse the Web with Microsoft's Internet Explorer

Microsoft Internet Explorer is quickly becoming a popular Web browser, especially for Windows 95 users. Although Internet Explorer does not yet support all the features that Netscape does, Microsoft is quickly closing the gap between the two products. One of the best features of Internet Explorer is that it's free.

 Microsoft Internet Explorer comes included in the Windows 95 Plus! Pack and comes pre-bundled on most new PC systems. Chances are that if you're running Windows 95, you already have Internet Explorer. However, the latest version, 2.0, is available for download directly from Microsoft's Web site at http://www.microsoft.com/windows/ie/iexplorer.htm.

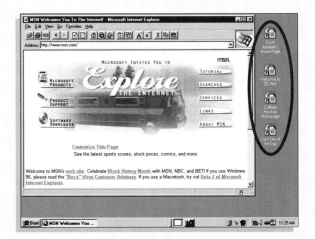

 You don't have to limit your URL shortcuts to the Favorites folder. Because Internet Explorer is tightly integrated with Windows 95, you can place your URL shortcuts almost anywhere, including the Windows 95 desktop. You can drag a shortcut into the Internet Explorer window to go immediately to that site. If Internet Explorer isn't running, you can double-click on any URL shortcut to launch Internet Explorer and navigate directly to that site.

Navigation buttons

Return to your home page

Reload the current page

Adjust the default font size

2 Internet Explorer has a simple toolbar for Web navigation and access to basic functions, such as printing and cut and paste capabilities. The arrow buttons allow you to browse through Web pages you've already visited in the current session. The font control buttons allow you to quickly adjust the size of the default font for better readability.

3 You can type in the URL in the address bar to instantly jump to any location on the Web. The address bar maintains a list of recently visited sites, which is accessible by clicking on the small arrow to the right of the bar. You can also jump to a new location by pressing Ctrl+O, choosing the Open Folder icon on the Toolbar, or by selecting Open from the File menu.

This is a Hyperlink.

4 Hyperlinks allow you to jump to another page on the Web. Internet Explorer displays hyperlinks in blue underlined text. When you pass the cursor over hyperlink text, it changes from the default arrow to a picture of a hand.

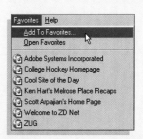

6 You can edit and maintain your list by choosing Open Favorites from the Favorites menu. Each URL in your Favorites list is a shortcut. You can add, edit, and delete your shortcuts, and even create subfolders to organize them. The Favorites folder works just like a Windows 95 Explorer window and supports drag and drop and right-click menus.

5 You can store your most frequently visited Web sites in the Internet Explorer Favorites list. To add the current site to your list of Favorites, choose Add to Favorites from the Favorites menu.

How to Browse the Web with Microsoft's Internet Explorer (Continued)

▶ **8** Internet Explorer supports context-sensitive menus. If you right-click your mouse in the browser window, you'll have quick access to special features.

12 Internet Explorer also supports a VRML (Virtual Reality Modeling Language) with a special add-in. This allows you to browse VRML sites, which are simulated 3-D worlds. You can use the keyboard arrows or drag your mouse cursor to walk around in a VRML world. A toolbar at the bottom of the VRML window provides additional navigation options. You can download the VRML add-in from the Internet Explorer home page at http://www.msn.com/ie/ie.htm.

TIP SHEET

▶ The current version of Internet Explorer is 2.0. The version that comes with Windows 95 and the Windows 95 Plus!Pack is 1.0. The new version contains many new features and enhancements. If you have not upgraded yet, be sure to visit the Internet Explorer home page and download the latest version.

9 Internet Explorer does not have its own built-in e-mail software. Instead, it supports sending e-mail through Microsoft Exchange, a separate software program which comes with Windows 95. If you have Microsoft Exchange installed, you can send e-mail by clicking on the Envelope icon on the toolbar, or by choosing Send from the File menu. By default, Exchange will include a shortcut and the URL of the active Web page in the body of the e-mail message.

10 Internet Explorer allows you to read Usenet newsgroups. You must have an Internet Provider that operates a newsgroup server running the NNTP news protocol (the Microsoft Network does not support NNTP). To access the newsgroups, choose Read Newsgroups from the Go menu.

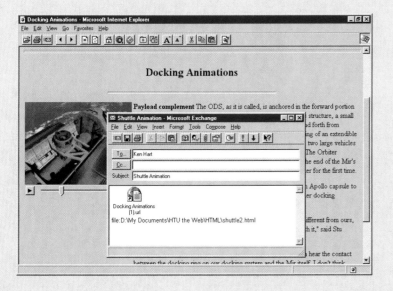

11 With Internet Explorer, you can watch AVI video files that are embedded inside Web pages. Internet Explorer provides basic playback controls so that you can pause, stop, and replay the video.

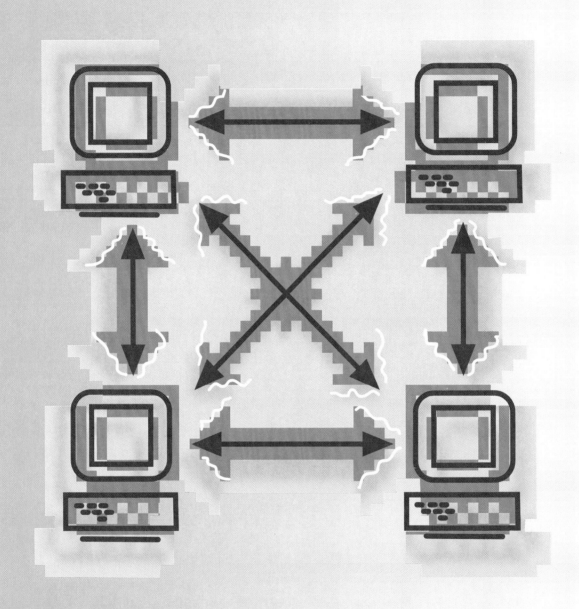

CHAPTER 5

Web Surfing with Online Services

 Web traffic has increased rapidly through commercial online services. America Online, CompuServe, and Prodigy have all opened up their doors to the Internet and now provide extensive access to the World Wide Web.

Getting up and running on the Web via one of the commercial online services is typically easy, especially for novices. Although the Web browsers the online services provide aren't as sophisticated as Netscape, Internet Explorer, or NCSA Mosaic, they're certainly adequate for the first-time Web surfer.

This chapter will introduce you to the Web browsers provided by three of the major online services: America Online, CompuServe, and Prodigy. You'll learn about the features and limitations found in each. The best part about browsing the Web via an online service is that very little setup is required. If you're already a member of one of these three online services, you'll be surfing the Web in a matter of minutes.

How to Browse the Web with America Online

If you're an America Online (AOL) user, accessing the Web is easy through AOL's bare-bones Web browser. Although this browser is primitive and lacks many of the features of the leading Web browsers, it is straightforward and simple to use. Best of all, it works entirely in conjunction with your existing AOL software, so no additional setup is required.

TIP SHEET

▶ **AOL offers free versions of their software that you can use for a trial period to explore their offerings and determine whether you wish to become a subscriber. AOL will mail you a complete software package, along with installation instructions. Call 1-800-827-3338 to receive the free trial software.**

▶ **If you're having trouble with the AOL Web browser, or just want to find out more about it, explore the Internet Connection area on AOL. The Internet Connection has numerous files, help documents, and question and answer forums dedicated to helping AOL users surf the Web. Click on the Internet Connection button in the AOL Main menu or use the keyword Internet.**

▶ **1** To browse the Web with AOL, you need version 2.5 or later of the AOL software. To download the latest version, use the keyword Upgrade, and follow the directions provided by AOL for upgrading your software.

8 You can change several options in the AOL Web browser by clicking on the Preferences button on the toolbar. To speed up the display of Web pages, for example, you can choose to not display graphics. You can also set the URL for your home page in the Preferences window.

 7 To add the current Web page to your list of Favorite Places, click on the heart-shaped icon in the browser window title bar. You can also select Add to Favorite Places from the Window menu.

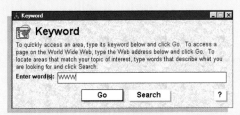

2 Connect to AOL as usual. Once connected, you can access the Web browser by using the keyword WWW, or by selecting the Internet Connection button from the Main menu.

3 AOL's Web browser has a very simple toolbar to help you navigate the Web. It includes buttons for moving backward and forward through pages you've visited, a button to reload the current page, and a button to take you back to your home page.

4 You can navigate to any site on the Web by typing its URL in the Location box and pressing Enter. If you click on the small arrow at the right of the Location box, you'll see a list of URLs for Web pages that you recently visited.

5 Hyperlinks allow you to jump to another page on the Web. AOL's Web browser displays hyperlinks in underlined blue text. In addition, when you pass the cursor over hyperlink text, it changes from the default arrow to a picture of a pointing hand.

6 The AOL Web browser lets you keep a list of your favorite Web sites for easy access. To access the list, click on the Favorite Places button on the toolbar. You can double-click on any item or drag and drop it into the browser window to navigate directly to that site.

How to Browse the Web with CompuServe

If you're a CompuServe user, you can now access the Web with the latest version of WinCIM, the Windows edition of the CompuServe Information Manager. The new version of WinCIM is actually a collection of separate software programs that work together to offer both regular CompuServe access and World Wide Web browsing capabilities in one package. The latest version of WinCIM comes bundled with CompuServe Mosaic, a special version of the popular Mosaic Web browser. It also includes the CompuServe Dialer, a utility for dialing into CompuServe and establishing the required PPP dial-up connection to the Internet.

 1 To browse the Web with CompuServe, you need WinCIM, version 2.0.1 or later. WinCIM 2.0.1 contains all of the required software, including the CompuServe Mosaic browser and the CompuServe Dialer. To download the latest version, use the GO word WINCIM, and follow the directions provided by CompuServe for downloading and upgrading your software.

 You can send e-mail directly from the CompuServe Mosaic browser by selecting Mail from the Tools menu. Type in the recipient's Internet address, a subject, and the body of your e-mail message. Click on the Send button when you're finished to complete the e-mail.

TIP SHEET

▶ **CompuServe has several forums dedicated to technical support for both WinCIM and Internet access. You can type GO WCIMSUPPORT to get specific information on using WinCIM, CompuServe Mosaic, and the CompuServe Dialer for accessing the Web. The Internet Resource Forum (GO INETRES) also has information and downloadable files for enhancing your Web browsing on CompuServe.**

 You can keep a list of your favorite Web sites by using CompuServe Mosaic's Hotlists. To access your Hotlists, click on the Hotlists button on the toolbar or press Ctrl+L on your keyboard. From the Hotlists window, you can double-click on any item to navigate directly to that site. To add the current Web page to your list of Favorite Places, click on the Add button.

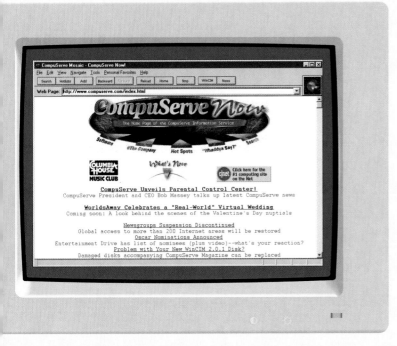

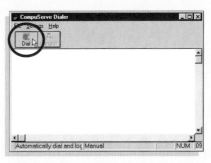

3 Click on the Dial button located on the tool-bar to connect to the CompuServe network and establish your PPP Internet connection.

2 Once you have installed the software, you can initiate your Internet connection with the CompuServe Dialer. Click on the Start button and select CompuServe Dialer from the CompuServe folder to launch the program. You can also double-click on the icon for CID.EXE, which will be located in the CID folder, inside your main CompuServe folder. If you accepted the installation defaults, the directory path should be C:\CSERVE\CID.

4 To launch the CompuServe Mosaic browser, click on the Start button and choose CompuServe Mosaic, which is located in the same folder as the CompuServe Dialer. CompuServe Mosaic will open up to your predefined home page.

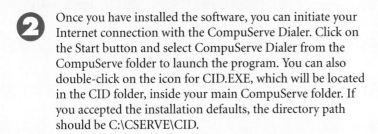

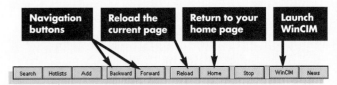

5 CompuServe Mosaic has a very simple toolbar to help you navigate the Web. It includes buttons for moving backward and forward through pages you've visited, a button to reload the current page, and a button to take you back to your home page. You can also launch WinCIM to access the CompuServe service while maintaining your Internet connection. This way, you can browse both CompuServe and the Web at the same time.

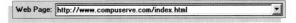

7 Hyperlinks allow you to jump to another page on the Web. By default, the CompuServe Mosaic browser displays hyperlinks in underlined blue text. In addition, when you pass the cursor over hyperlink text, it changes from the default arrow to a picture of a pointing hand.

6 You can navigate to any site on the Web by typing its URL in the Web page box and pressing Enter. If you click on the small arrow at the right of the Web Page box, you'll see a list of URLs for sites that you recently visited.

How to Browse the Web with Prodigy

If you're a Prodigy subscriber, Web access is easy. If the newest version of the software is installed, no additional setup is necessary. You'll be browsing the Web in a matter of minutes.

1 To browse the Web with Prodigy, you must have the new Prodigy for Windows software, version 1.1 or later. If you haven't upgraded your software yet, you can type **JUMP UPGRADE** to download the new version.

7 To send an e-mail message from within the Prodigy browser, choose Send E-Mail from the Navigate menu. Type in the recipient's e-mail address, a subject, and the body of your message. When you're finished typing, click on the Send button.

6 The Prodigy Web browser uses Hot Lists to give you instant access to your favorite Web sites. To access the list, click on the Hot List button on the toolbar or choose Hot Lists from the Navigate menu. You can double-click on any item to navigate directly to that site. Click on the Add to Hot List button to place the current Web page in your list.

TIP SHEET

▶ **You can browse the Web and use the regular Prodigy service at the same time. The two programs run as separate tasks on your computer, although they share the same phone connection. You can switch between the Prodigy Web browser and the regular Prodigy software using the Task Bar or by pressing Alt+Tab.**

2 After installing the new software, launch Prodigy. Enter your user ID and password in the Sign-On screen. Choose Web Browser as your destination and hit the Connect button to sign on to Prodigy. Once connected, choose Browse the Web from the main screen. The Prodigy Web browser will launch, and you'll be on the World Wide Web.

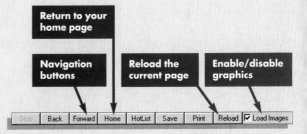

Return to your home page

Navigation buttons

Reload the current page

Enable/disable graphics

3 Like most Web browsers, the Prodigy browser features a basic toolbar to help you navigate the Web. It includes buttons for moving backward and forward through pages you've visited, a button to reload the current page and a button to take you back to your home page. If you deselect the Load Images box, Web pages will load faster, but you won't see any graphics.

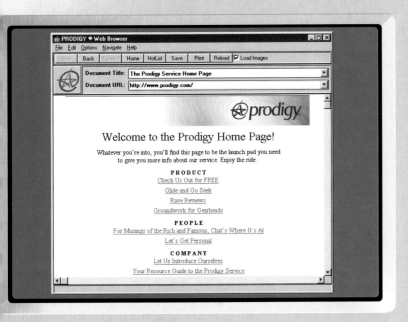

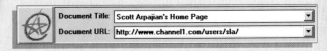

4 You can navigate to any site on the Web by typing its URL in the Document URL box and pressing Enter. If you click on the small arrow at the right of the Document URL box, you'll see a list of URLs for Web pages that you recently visited. You can also navigate to a page you've already visited by selecting it from the Document Title drop-down list.

5 Hyperlinks allow you to jump to another page on the Web. Prodigy's Web browser displays hyperlinks in underlined blue text. In addition, when you pass the cursor over hyperlink text, it changes from the default arrow to a picture of a hand.

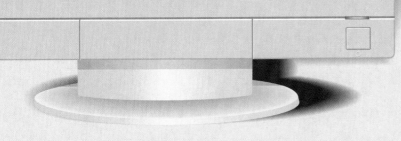

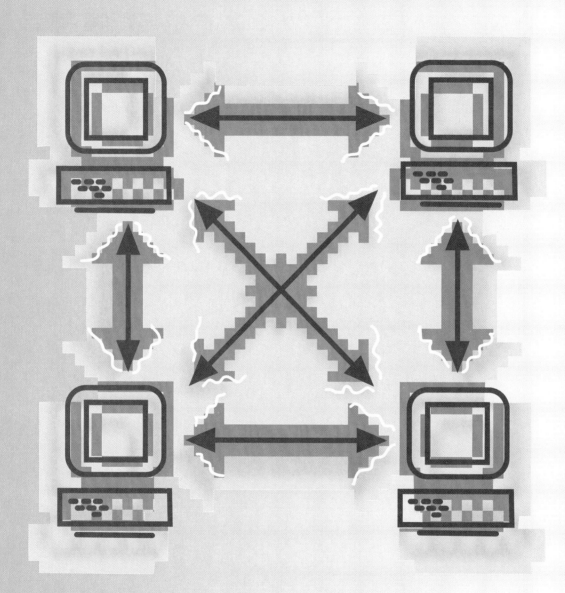

CHAPTER 6

Using Helper Applications

Although Netscape, NCSA, and others are constantly updating the capabilities of their Web browsers, certain audio files, images, video clips, and other multimedia elements may be impossible for your browser to open. In such situations, you will need to use a *helper application*. A helper application is a program that can display a particular type of file, and these helper applications are usually used to view or play images, movies, and sound clips. A helper application is launched by your Web browser, but it is not part of the browser—you need to acquire the helper application yourself and then configure your browser to automatically launch the application whenever it needs to display a particular type of file.

Finding helper applications on the Web is a fairly straightforward process. Both NCSA and Netscape maintain Web pages outlining the functions and costs of several popular helper applications, with links for downloading them directly.

This chapter will introduce you to some of the most popular helper applications, showing you how to use them and where they can be found.

How to Find Helper Applications on the Web

Throughout this chapter, we have listed the URLs of some of the best helper applications available. However, there are many different helper applications available for each type of file, and that means there are plenty of choices available. In this section, you'll learn about some of the best sites available for downloading helper applications and finding the ones that are best for you.

▶ **①** A good first stop is always either the Netscape or NCSA Mosaic helper applications pages; both list nearly all the helper applications presented in this chapter. They also contain links to a few others that might work as well, depending on your particular Web browser and computer setup. Netscape's Helper application page is at http://home.netscape.com/assist/helper_apps/index.html.

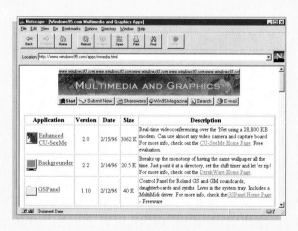

⑤ One of the best sites for Windows 95 users is Windows 95.com. This site maintains an extensive list of downloadable 32-bit software, optimized for Windows 95 and NT. For a complete list of graphics and multimedia helper applications, point your Web browser to http://www.windows95.com/apps/mmedia.html.

TIP SHEET

▶ The Web is the easiest place to find helper applications, but it's not the only place where you can find them. Compu-Serve's Internet Resources Forum (GO INETRES) has a large collection of helper applications. You can also browse the NCSA Mosaic FTP site at ftp://ftp.ncsa.uiuc.edu/Mosaic/Windows/.

▶ Most of the helper applications available on the Web are either completely free or are offered as shareware. Shareware is a way of marketing software that allows you to try the program before you commit to purchasing it. You can download and use the program for a trial period, but you are obligated to pay for the program if you decide to keep it. Each shareware program has its own terms and license for use. Consult the program's documentation for specific details.

2 The NCSA Mosaic page also has an extensive list of helper applications, and offers some background information on the technology behind the process. The URL is http://www.ncsa.uiuc.edu/SDG/Software/WinMosaic/viewers.html.

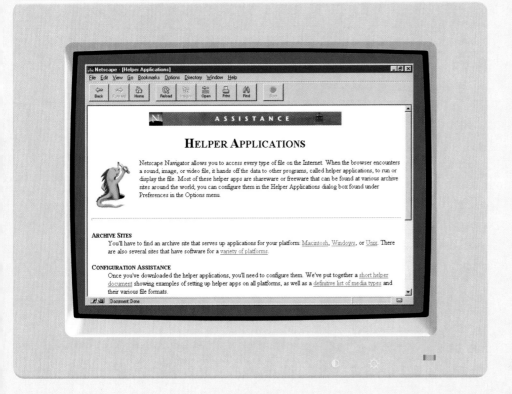

3 Yahoo! maintains an extensive database of helper applications for almost all file types and operating systems. The URL for the helper applications page at Yahoo! is http://www.yahoo.com/Computers_and_Internet/Internet/World_Wide_Web/Browsers/Helper_Applications/.

4 Another page full of links to the most popular helper applications is maintained by the University of California at San Diego. The URL for the page is http://ssdc.ucsd.edu/dt/helpers.html.

How to Install a Helper Application in Netscape

I n this section, you'll learn how to configure a helper application with Netscape.

Most of the files you'll encounter on the Web are of the MIME type. MIME is short for Multiple Internet Mail Extension, and is a standard method of identifying a file format on the Internet. MIME types consist of two parts: a main type and a subtype. For example, the MIME type for a .GIF file is image/gif. Likewise, the MIME type for a Microsoft Word document is application/msword. Fortunately, that's about all you really need to know about MIME types.

Most browsers use a file's MIME type to determine which helper application to launch. If the browser can't handle a particular MIME type on its own, it checks to see if you've identified a helper application for viewing that particular MIME type. If one is found, the helper application is launched.

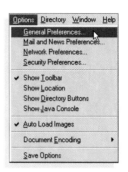

 1 Launch Netscape and then select General Preferences from the Options menu.

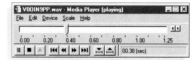

7 The next time you click on a link to a .WAV sound file, Netscape will launch the Windows Media Player. Media Player will then play the .WAV file.

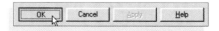

6 Click on the OK button when you're finished to return to the main Netscape window.

TIP SHEET

▶ **If you'd like to delve deeper into the world of MIME types, point your Web browser to http://home.netscape.com/assist/helper_ apps/mime. html. You'll discover everything you could possibly want to know about the MIME classification system.**

▶ **Almost all of the Windows helper applications on the Web are compressed in ZIP archives. One of the best programs available for handling ZIP files is WinZip, a shareware program. You can download the evaluation version of WinZip from the WinZip home page at http://www. winzip.com.**

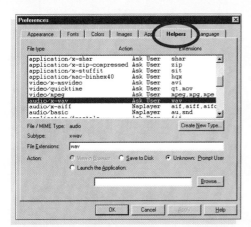

2 In the Preferences window, select the Helpers tab and scroll down until you see the file type audio/x-wav. This is the MIME classification for a .WAV sound file.

3 By default, the action for this type of file is set to Unknown: Prompt User. This means that Netscape will normally prompt you with a dialog box asking you to pick a viewer or save the file to disk whenever it encounters a .WAV file on the Web.

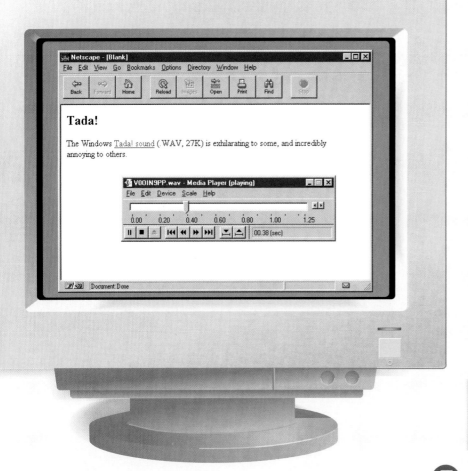

4 Change the action to Launch the Application by clicking inside the radio button next to that option.

5 In the text box, type **c:\windows\mplayer .exe**. This is the full path name to the Windows Media Player program. You can also click on the browse button to find the appropriate application using the Windows Explorer.

How to Use Graphics Helper Applications

A browser's primary responsibility is to provide you with a means for exploring the Web. Once you are happily cruising around, however, you may bump into certain types of graphic files on the Web that your browser is not capable of viewing. Most browsers, including Netscape and NCSA Mosaic, can handle all the commonly used graphic file formats, but additional helper applications are available to handle to more obscure ones. If you have a versatile and complete helper application installed, your Web journey will run all the more smoothly.

In this section, you'll learn how to find and configure a helper application for viewing Tagged Image Format files (.TIF) with Netscape.

7 Paint Shop Pro is now configured as a helper application for viewing .TIF image files. The next time Netscape comes across a .TIF file on the Web, it will download it and launch Paint Shop Pro to view the image.

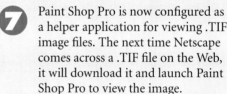

6 In the Action field, select the option Launch the Application. In the text box below that, type in the full path name to Paint Shop Pro. You can also use the Browse button to locate Paint Shop Pro if you're uncertain of the exact path name. When you're finished, click on the OK button to return to Netscape.

TIP SHEET

▶ **Paint Shop Pro handles many different graphics formats. You can repeat steps 4–7 for each of the different graphics formats you need to view.**

▶ **If you want to learn more about graphics on the Web, turn to Excite's listing of Computer Graphics sites at http://www.excite.com/ Subject/Computing/Graphics/ s-index.h.html.**

In-line images

External image

1 Images on the Web are classified into two types: in-line and external. In-line images are meant to be part of a larger Web document. The bullets, icons, and small graphics that you see on a Web page are examples of in-line images. External images are available via hyperlinks, and are intended to be viewed separately from the Web page.

2 Most Web designers create their pages using in-line image formats that are widely supported by browsers, so that helper applications are not necessary for viewing the main Web pages. However, external images may be provided in less common formats, and therefore may require a helper application to view them.

3 One of the best helper applications for viewing graphics under Windows 95 is Paint Shop Pro, a shareware program. Paint Shop Pro is a complete image viewer and editor that supports over 30 different file formats. An evaluation version is available for downloading from the Paint Shop Pro home page at http://www.jasc.com/.

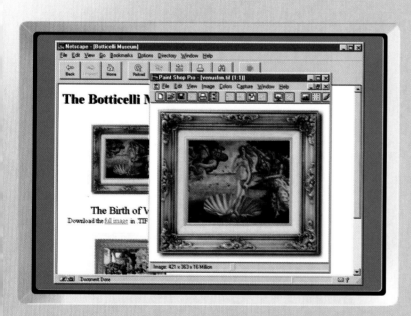

4 After you have downloaded and installed Paint Shop Pro on your system, you need to configure it as a helper application for your browser. In Netscape, select General Preferences from the Options menu and then click on the Helpers tab.

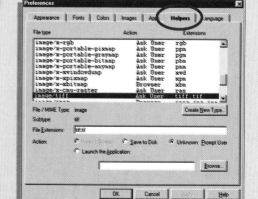

5 Scroll down until you see the file type image/tiff. This is the MIME classification for a .TIF image file.

How to Use Audio Helper Applications

Audio helper applications work on the same principle as graphics helper applications. They handle file formats that the browser is not capable of playing on its own. Sound files on the Web are usually found in one of two formats: .WAV and .AU. The .WAV file format is common and should be familiar to Windows users. The .AU format is a popular file format for the UNIX system, and is very common on the Internet. You may also encounter less common sound file formats in your travels on the Web.

▶ ❶ One of the most versatile utilities for listening to sound clips in Windows 95 is Cool Edit from Syntrillium Software Corporation. This shareware program is a full-featured sound player and editor. It can handle most of the sound file formats that you'll encounter on the World Wide Web. You can download Cool Edit from Syntrillium Software's home page at http://www.netzone.com/syntrillium/.

❻ Cool Edit is now configured as a helper application for listening to .AU sound files. When you encounter a sound clip in .AU format, Netscape will launch Cool Edit with the sound clip loaded and ready to play.

TIP SHEET

▶ You can configure Cool Edit to be a helper application for .WAV files as well by repeating steps 2–6.

2 After you have installed Cool Edit on your system, you're ready to configure it as a helper application for your browser. In Netscape, select General Preferences from the Options menu.

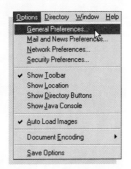

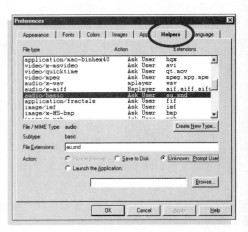

3 Click on the Helpers tab and then select the file type audio/basic. This is the MIME classification for the SUN/Next .AU sound format, which is extremely common on the Web.

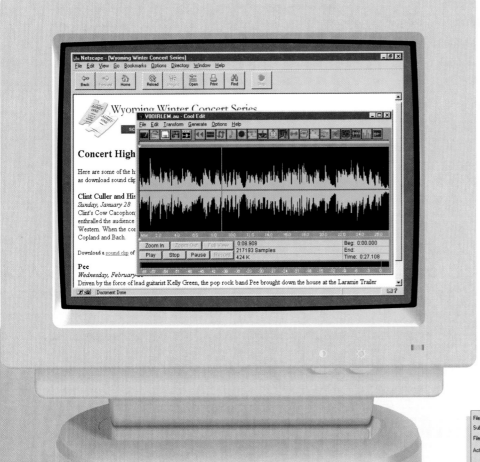

4 In the Action field, select the option Launch the Application. Depending on how you installed Netscape, this option may already be selected. In the text box below, type in the full path name to Cool Edit. You can also use the Browse button to locate Cool Edit if you're uncertain of the exact path name.

5 Click on the OK button to return to Netscape.

How to Use Video and Multimedia Helper Applications

Already you can find thousands of video clips on the Web, and the number of sites integrating video into their presentation is growing. Unfortunately, few Web browsers are capable of playing video and multimedia files on their own. To fully experience all the multimedia content that the Web has to offer, you'll need a helper application.

Two of the most common multimedia file formats on the Web today are QuickTime and MPEG. QuickTime is a popular movie format developed by Apple Computer originally for use on the Macintosh computer. The popularity of the format drove Apple to create a Windows version of the QuickTime movie player.

MPEG is a video standard outlined by the Motion Pictures Experts Group. It is well known for its excellent compression ratios, which means that the video files are relatively small, making them ideal for downloading from the Internet. Because MPEG is not proprietary, there are many viewers available.

TIP SHEET

▶ Several Web sites have large collections of videos. One of the best is NASA's gallery of space movies. You can access it from the NASA home page at http://www.nasa.gov/.

▶ **1** You can download the Windows version of the QuickTime player for free from Apple's Web site at http://quicktime.apple.com/. It is available in both 16-bit (for Windows 3.1) and 32-bit (for Windows 95) versions.

9 Click on the OK button to return to Netscape. Netscape is now configured to launch VMPEG when it downloads an MPEG movie on the Web.

8 Highlight the file type video/mpeg. In the Action field, select Launch Application. Then, type in the full path name to the VMPEG viewer in the text box.

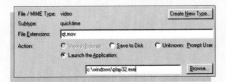

2 After installing QuickTime, choose General Preferences from the Options menu. Then click on the Helpers tab and select the file type video/quicktime.

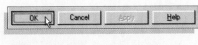

3 In the Action field, choose Launch Application and then type in the path name to the QuickTime player in the text box. By default, QuickTime installs itself into your Windows directory. If you installed the 32-bit version of QuickTime, the full path name should be c:\windows\ play32.exe.

4 Click on the OK button to return to Netscape.

5 Netscape is now configured to launch the QuickTime movie player whenever it encounters a QuickTime movie on the Web.

7 After you install VMPEG, select General Preferences from Netscape's Options menu and click on the Helpers tab.

6 VMPEG is one of the more popular MPEG movie viewers available on the Internet. A free evaluation version of the program is available at many FTP sites, including ftp://papa.indstate.edu/winsock-l/Windows95/Graphics/vmpeg17.exe.

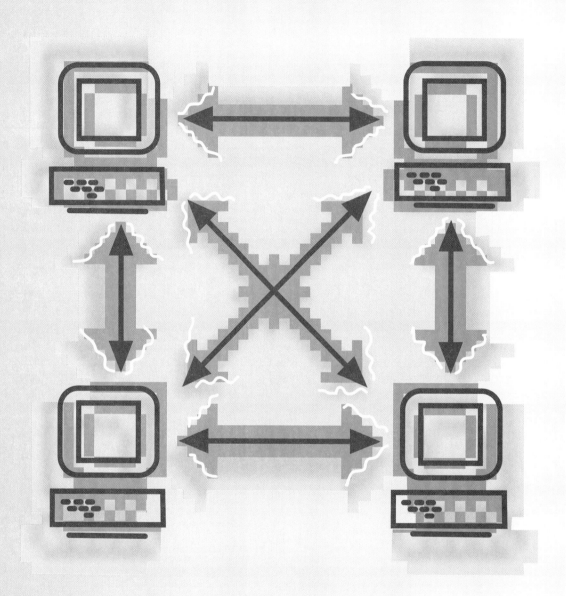

CHAPTER 7

Finding It on the Web: Web Searching and Navigation

 Fruitful searches at the library often start with a visit to the card catalog. It works the same way with the Web. Although there is no complete and comprehensive catalog of every Web site, there are many helpful references that can save you time and make your foray into the Web more productive.

Of course, unlike the local library, the Web is not neatly organized into categorized sections, and there's no Dewey Decimal system to guide you. Fortunately, there are many good catalog resources that attempt to categorize as much of the Web as possible. Several of these Web site directories are divided, subdivided, cross-referenced, and indexed by every imaginable scheme. You can find indexes that are sorted alphabetically by topic, or just broken down into logical categories with further layers of subcategories.

If all this seems to take the fun out of the anarchy of the Web, take heart. New Web sites that haven't yet been discovered and cataloged pop up in ever increasing numbers each day, while the old resources change or die away. By using some of the search tools outlined in this chapter, you can do quite a bit of exploring on your own, and possibly be one of the first to discover tomorrow's cool new site.

How to Find Search Tools and Navigation Aids

Once you have found one navigation aid on the Web, chances are you have found them all, or at least all the well-known ones. All of the most popular navigation resources have sections with hyperlinks to the other prominent resources.

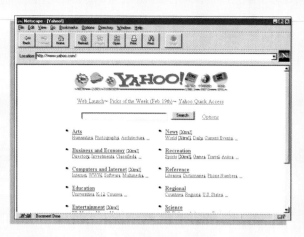

1 The first comprehensive directory for the World Wide Web was Yahoo. Although it sounds like the silly call of a happy cowboy, this little resource ranch has made quite a name for itself out on the wild Web frontier. In the next section, you'll get the details on how to use Yahoo. If you'd like to take a quick peek right away, saddle up your Web browser and mosey on over to http://www.yahoo.com.

TIP SHEET

▶ In some cases, these resources will list more than just Web sites. The hierarchical databases will often have sections for FTP sites, Usenet newsgroups, gopher sites, and more.

▶ Some search engines have resources that point to "cool sites" or "sites of the week." These are worth exploring because they are specifically picked by people who review literally hundreds of sites each day.

5 As you can probably tell from these examples, there are two basic types of navigation aids on the Web: search indexes (also called search engines) and hierarchical directories (basically lists of lists, or phone books for the Web). You can use both equally to your advantage depending on what you're looking for.

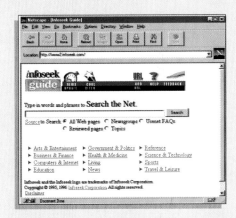

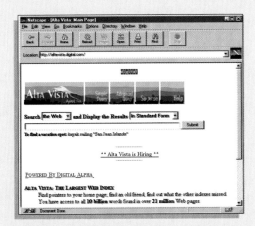

2 The Web is big enough for more than one directory, especially if the people that created WebCrawler have anything to say about it. WebCrawler will be covered in more detail later in this chapter. Like Yahoo, this resource is worth a quick look right now. Plug the following URL into your browser's location entry box and take a look: http://www.webcrawler.com.

3 The next recommended navigation resource is called InfoSeek Guide. InfoSeek is primarily a search engine. Check it out by navigating your browser to http://guide.infoseek.com.

4 You can access the home page of Digital Alta Vista search engine by pointing your browser to http://www.altavista.digital.com/.

How to Use Yahoo

Yahoo is clearly one of the most popular search tools on the Web. Like the other popular navigation resources, it offers both the user-defined seek-and-retrieve–style search and an extensive subject list indexed by category. Another aspect that has helped this resource become so popular is that it is as easy to use as it is to remember.

TIP SHEET

▸ **Yahoo provides a list of additional search engines on the Web. You can find the list at the bottom of the Search page at http://www.yahoo.com/search.html.**

▸ **Yahoo also provides a lengthy list of Web and Internet search resources. Follow the Yahoo directory path Computers and Internet: Internet: World Wide Web: Searching the Web.**

▶ **1** Start at the Yahoo home page by typing in the URL http://www.yahoo.com into your browser's location entry box.

8 Yahoo will then return a list of matches based on the information you supplied. If you click on any of the hyperlinks that Yahoo provides, you'll be taken either to a new Web site or to a list of sites in the Yahoo directory.

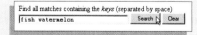

7 Enter a word or words to search for in the text entry box and then click on the Search button. Yahoo will take a few moments to process your request.

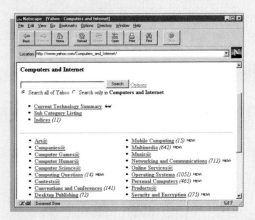

2 To navigate through the Yahoo site using its basic hierarchical directory, first pick a topic. This will show you a list of lists that fall under a general heading. A good example is the category of Computers and Internet. Click on the link.

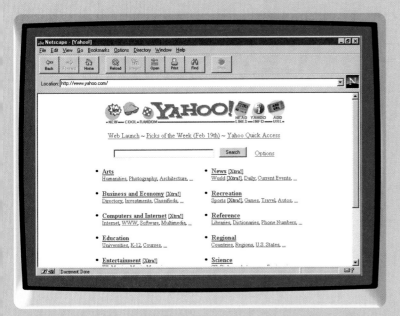

3 This will take you to a listing of subcategories under the Computers and Internet heading. As you continue to move from the general to the specific, you will see the path of your category search displayed at the top of the window. Follow any path of your choice to view the Web sites listed.

4 Return to the Yahoo home page by clicking on the word Yahoo at the top of the screen.

5 The next feature to try is the fill-in form search. You can type a keyword in the text entry box, and Yahoo will search its database of Web pages looking for matches. You can also have Yahoo perform a more detailed search by clicking on the Options link to the right of the search button. Click on it now to customize your search parameters.

6 Using this page, you can control your search. If you want to enter more than one keyword, you can specify whether Yahoo looks for documents containing any one of the keywords, or only documents that contain all of the keywords together. Another setting allows you to specify whether Yahoo should consider the keywords you entered to be parts of words or complete words. You can also limit the number of matches Yahoo returns at a time. The default setting is 25.

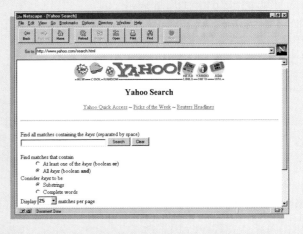

How to Use WebCrawler

Whereas Yahoo offers both a user-entry search tool and a hierarchical subject directory, WebCrawler focuses primarily on the user-entry search engine alone. The interface is clear and straightforward, presenting a basic entry window to type in your search request, and two simple delimiter menus to further define your search.

1 Start at the WebCrawler home page. Point your browser to http://www.webcrawler.com.

6 The best way to become familiar with this search tool is to just play around with it a bit. You may find some surprising results from some fairly ordinary-looking search queries—it all depends on the words you plug in.

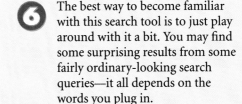

5 Notice too that there is a column of numbers running down the left side of the returned search results. These numbers represent the level of relevance that the returned site has to your search query, rated on a scale from 1 to 100. These numbers are calculated based on the total number of words on the page found versus the number of words found from your search query.

TIP SHEET

▶ **WebCrawler includes a handy Help link off the front page that further explains how to get the best results from your search requests. It includes examples of various searches and results as well as a list of the most frequently asked questions (or FAQs), and the answers to those questions.**

▶ **WebCrawler's main search tool is called a forms-based search engine because it requires a forms-compatible browser such as Netscape or NCSA Mosaic. If your browser doesn't support forms, you can still use the WebCrawler search function at the following alternative URL: http://www.webcrawler.com/ cgi-bin/WebQuery.**

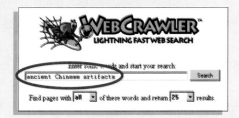

2 Enter some keywords for WebCrawler to search on. Try entering several words to see how WebCrawler interprets your request. For example, type the words **ancient Chinese artifacts** into the text entry box.

3 You can further clarify your search request with the any/all option. To search for documents that contain all the keywords together, make sure that the option is set to *all*. To return documents with at least one of the keywords, set the option to *any*. You can also select the maximum number of results you'd like to receive. The default is 25, but you may choose to receive 10 or 100 results instead. When you're ready, click on the Search button to see what happens.

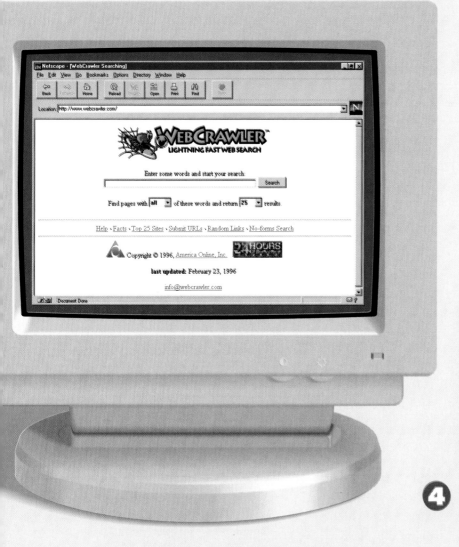

4 As you can see, WebCrawler quickly returns several results that fit the above search criteria. If you selected the *all* option when you performed the search, then each of these documents contains all the keywords you specified in the text entry box. Note that this does not mean that all three words are combined as a complete phrase; it just means that each of these Web documents contains all three words somewhere in the main body of text.

How to Use InfoSeek Guide

InfoSeek Guide is a popular service for searching the Web. The heart of InfoSeek Guide is a powerful and comprehensive search engine coupled with one of the most extensive databases of Web pages on the Internet. InfoSeek Guide used to be a subscriber-only service, but now it is available free of charge.

1 Go to the InfoSeek Guide front page at http://guide.infoseek.com.

8 You can learn even more about refining your search by visiting InfoSeek Guide's Search Tips page at http://guide.infoseek.com/IS/Help?SearchHelp.html.

TIP SHEET

▶ **InfoSeek Guide has a handy Help page with further information about how to use InfoSeek's search tools. This page can be accessed by selecting Help from the InfoSeek toolbar.**

▶ **InfoSeek Corporation offers a separate subscription service called InfoSeek Professional. This service lets you search through several databases for information such as news stories, competitor's financial statements, and market research reports. You can get more information on the service by visiting the InfoSeek professional home page at http://professional.infoseek.com/Home.**

7 If certain words need to appear in the document but the specific order does not matter, preface them with a plus sign. For example, to search for documents that must contain the word cheese, and may also contain the words eggs and milk, type **+cheese milk eggs** in the text entry box.

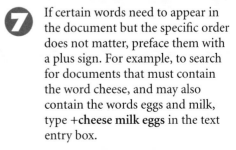

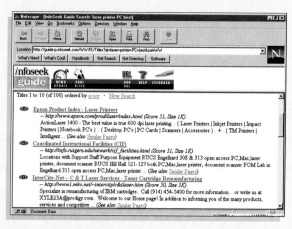

2 You can enter keywords to search on in the text entry box. For example, to search for information on the best laser printers for the PC, you might type **laser printer PC best**.

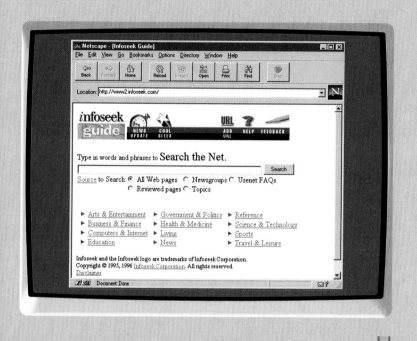

3 InfoSeek Guide measures the frequency of the keywords you specified contained in the documents in its database and sends up to 100 results, sorted by relevance.

4 InfoSeek also maintains a directory called Topics to help you find a particular subject area. You can navigate through the Topic section and its subtopics, and then perform a search within that topic to get better search results. You can also locate Web pages simply by browsing through the topics until you find a particular page description that interests you.

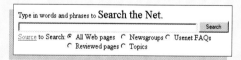

5 You can limit your search to different types of documents using the Source field. Normally, InfoSeek Guide will search all of its known Web documents. However, you can force InfoSeek Guide to look only in Usenet newsgroup postings, FAQs, or within a subset of Web pages that the staff at InfoSeek has reviewed. You can also select Topics to search for a particular InfoSeek Guide Topics page.

6 You can modify the keywords you type in to further refine your search. For example, to search on an exact phrase, enclose your keywords in quotes. For example, if you type **cow jumped over the moon**, InfoSeek will return documents containing any of the five words. However, if you enclose the keyword phrase in quotes, InfoSeek Guide will only return documents with all of those words in the exact order that they appear.

How to Use Digital's Alta Vista

The Alta Vista search engine is a free service from Digital Equipment Corporation. It is one of the newest search services on the Web, and it boasts the most comprehensive database of Web pages available. It also features an impressive and flexible search query language, which makes it an ideal tool for power users on the Web.

▶ **1** Start at the Alta Vista home page. Point your browser to http://altavista.digital.com/.

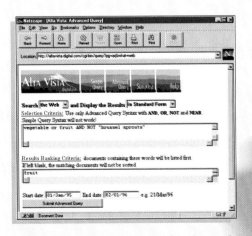

7 You can use Alta Vista's Advanced Query for more sophisticated searching. Click on the Advanced Query icon at the top of the page to access this section of Alta Vista. The Advanced Query gives you more control over your keyword searches, and allows you to determine how the search should weight the results. The Advanced Query uses a different syntax than the Simple Query. Complete instructions are available by clicking on the Help icon.

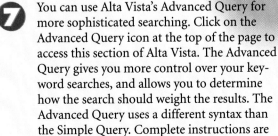

TIP SHEET

▶ Alta Vista's Surprise icon will take you on a random jump to somewhere else on the Web. Click on the Surprise icon and then select a category. You'll instantly be taken to one of the millions of Web pages in Alta Vista's database.

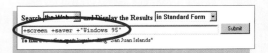

2 Alta Vista supports two search types: a simple and an advanced search. Most of the time you'll want to perform the default simple search. First, enter the keywords for your search in the text entry box. For example, to search the Web for information on screen savers for Windows 95, you might type **screen saver Windows 95**.

3 After just a few moments, the Alta Vista search engine returns its results. As you'll notice, there are quite a few possibilities—perhaps more than 30,000 matches. That's because Alta Vista is looking for documents that contain any of your keywords. You can refine the search using the plus sign to indicate required words and quotation marks to mark phrases. For example, to refine the previous search, type **+screen +saver +"Windows 95"**. This will return only documents with all three search terms found.

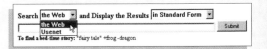

4 Using the drop-down selection boxes, you can choose to perform your search on either Web documents or Usenet newsgroups. You can also choose the type of display for your results, which can range from compact (single-line listings) to detailed form.

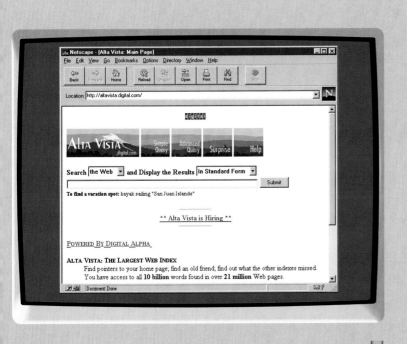

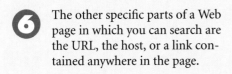

6 The other specific parts of a Web page in which you can search are the URL, the host, or a link contained anywhere in the page.

5 You can constrain your keyword searches to certain parts of a Web page. To perform such a search, type in a special prefix for the part of the page to search, followed by a colon and the keyword or phrase. For example, to search for the keyword *spam*, but only when it appears in the title of a Web page, type **title:spam** in the text entry box.

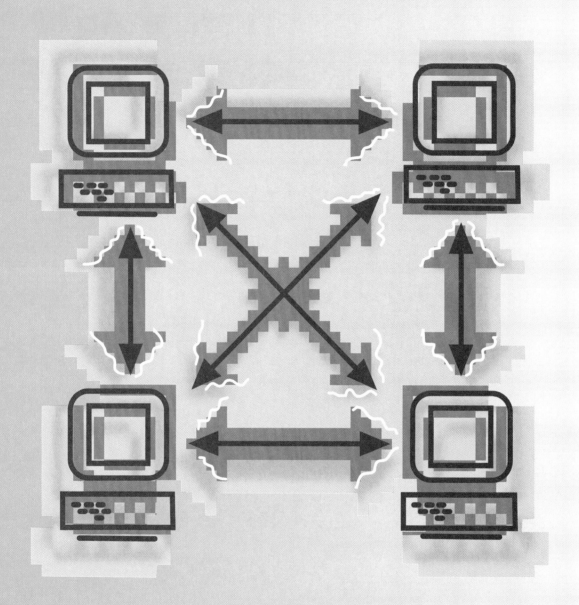

CHAPTER 8

Weaving a Wider Web: How to Access Other Parts of the Internet with Your Web Browser

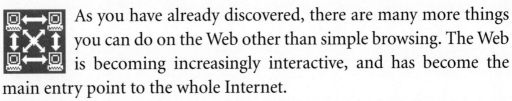 As you have already discovered, there are many more things you can do on the Web other than simple browsing. The Web is becoming increasingly interactive, and has become the main entry point to the whole Internet.

The most used elements of the Internet have to do with personal communications: e-mail, person-to-person chats (called IRC or Internet Relay Chat), Usenet newsgroups, and interactive games. Some of these resources can be accessed through your Web browser itself (depending on which browser you are using). All of these resources have pertinent information about them available on the Web, such as hints and tips, indexes for locating related resource information, and help for finding the applications you need to get at these resources if you aren't able to access them with your browser.

Currently, Netscape's Navigator version 2.0 is the only browser with fully functional e-mail and Usenet newsgroup access built in. This chapter will show how you can access some of these resources directly if you are using the Netscape Navigator 2.0 browser.

This chapter will also show you how you can use the Web to find other applications and helpful information on all these personal communications resources regardless of the Web browser you are using.

How to Use E-Mail with Netscape Navigator 2.0

The latest release of Netscape's Navigator contains a powerful e-mail program built in. It is tightly integrated with the Netscape browser, and provides a friendly and usable interface. The e-mail capabilities include all the standard functions you'd expect, and a personal address book for storing frequently used contact names. You can even embed Internet hyperlinks right into your messages, so that other Netscape Navigator users can follow links you provide via e-mail.

TIP SHEET

▶ You can use the Netscape Mail Address book to store frequently used e-mail addresses. You can also create e-mail groups. To save typing, you can assign nicknames to both individual e-mail addresses and groups. To open the Address Book, click on the Address icon in the toolbar of the message composition window, or select Address Book from the Window menu in the main Netscape Mail window.

▶ You can attach files and URL hyperlinks to e-mail messages by clicking on the Attach icon in the message composition window. If you send URL links to a recipient who is also using Netscape 2.0, the hyperlinked Web page will actually be displayed in the body of the e-mail message.

1 To use Netscape's e-mail features, you need to have an e-mail account with an Internet Service Provider with POP and SMTP servers. Check with your ISP beforehand. Your ISP will need to provide you with important information such as your user name, your password, and the addresses of the POP and SMTP servers.

8 Type a subject for your message in the Subject field, and then type the body of your message in the main text field. When you're finished with your message, click on the Send button or choose Send Now from the File menu. You can also press Ctrl+Enter to send the message.

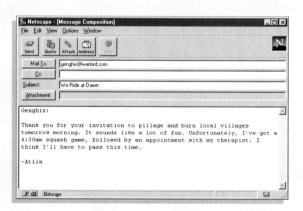

7 When you choose to create a new message, a message composition window appears. Type in the e-mail address of the recipient in the Mail To field. You can send mail to multiple recipients by separating each e-mail address with a comma. You can also send copies of the message by typing e-mail addresses in the cc: field.

6 To compose a new e-mail message, click on the button marked To:Mail, or choose New Mail Message from the File menu. You can also press Ctrl+M on the keyboard.

3 Select Netscape Mail from the Window menu to open the mail program.

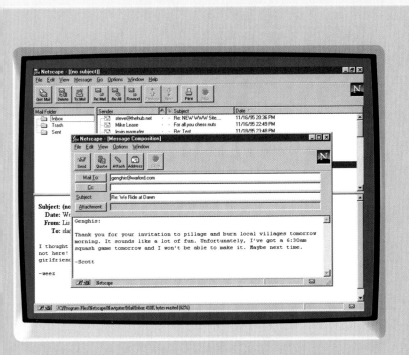

2 Configure your Netscape Navigator e-mail functions by selecting Mail and News Preferences from the Options menu. Then click on the Servers tab. Fill in the outgoing and incoming server addresses and the user name that your ISP provided for you. When you're finished, click the OK button to return to Netscape.

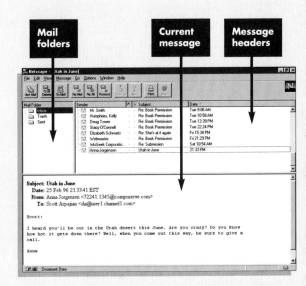

4 The Netscape e-mail window is divided into three frames. The top-left frame shows all of your mail folders, including your Inbox and a folder for mail that you have sent. The top-right frame provides a one-line summary of all the message headers in the current folder, including the name of the sender and the subject. The bottom frame is used to display the actual contents of the current mail message. You can resize each frame to suit your preferences by clicking a frame border and dragging it to the desired position.

5 The button bar at the top of the mail window gives you quick access to many common e-mail functions. Using the button bar, you can retrieve your waiting e-mail from the server, compose and delete messages, as well as reply to or forward the message you're currently reading. You can also scroll through your mail folder and print messages.

How to Access Usenet Newsgroups with Netscape Navigator

N etscape Navigator 2.0 is the first Web browser to fully integrate the Usenet newsgroup reading capabilities. Its newsgroup feature lets you sort and list messages from subscribed newsgroups, as well as access threaded news posts and articles.

1 Before you can use Netscape Navigator's newsgroup features, you need some configuration information from your Internet Service Provider. Your ISP needs to be running a news server that uses the NNTP news protocol. Check with your ISP beforehand and find out the name of the NNTP news server.

7 Compose your message in the provided window. You can post the same message to multiple newsgroups by separating each address with a comma in the newsgroups field. You can also send a copy of the posting to an individual by entering an e-mail address in the cc: field. When you're finished, click on the Send button to post the message.

6 To post a message to the newsgroup, click on the To:News button on the toolbar, or select New News Message from the File menu.

TIP SHEET

▶ **More information about Netscape's newsgroup features and functions is available online at the following URL: http://home.netscape.com/eng/mozilla/2.0/handbook/docs/mnb.html#CO, or to save the trouble of typing in the full URL, just select Handbook from Netscape's on-screen Help menu in the upper-right corner of the screen.**

▶ **Netscape's newsgroup feature allows you to embed pictures and other multimedia information in your postings. For more information on the Netscape Navigator features for version 2.0, visit the Netscape 2.0 features page at: http://home.netscape.com/comprod/products/navigator/version_2.0/.**

2 Configure your Netscape Navigator newsgroup functions by selecting Mail and News Preferences from the Options menu. Then click on the Servers tab. Fill in the NNTP news server name in the appropriate box. When you're finished, click the OK button to return to Netscape.

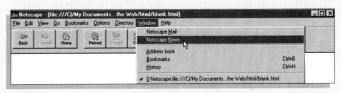

3 Select Netscape News from the Window menu to open the news reader.

Newsgroup message headers

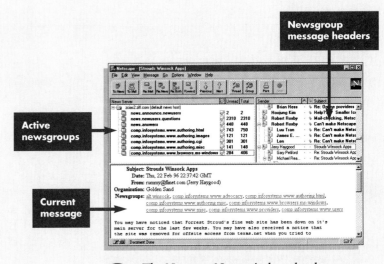

Active newsgroups

Current message

4 The Netscape News window closely resembles the Netscape Mail window, and is divided into three frames. The top-left frame shows available newsgroups. A check mark next to a newsgroup indicates that you have subscribed to it. The top-right frame provides a one-line summary of all the message headers in the current newsgroup. The headers are organized in a hierarchical tree, with replies appearing indented from the original message. The bottom frame displays the contents of the current message. You can resize each frame to suit your preferences by clicking a frame border and dragging it to the desired position.

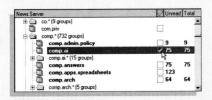

5 Adding newsgroups to your active list is simple. You can select Add Newsgroup from the File menu and type in the name of the newsgroup. You can also select Show All Newsgroups from the Options menu and then select the ones you want to subscribe to by marking them with a check mark in the corresponding box When you're finished, you can return to a simplified list by selecting Show Subscribed Newsgroups from the Options menu.

How to Chat with IRC

IRC, or Internet Relay Chat, is a popular way for people to talk to friends on the Internet. It works by allowing several users to connect together in specific chat areas, called channels. Once connected, users see live conversations taking place, and can participate by typing on their keyboards. In more ways than one, IRC is quickly becoming the CB radio of the nineties.

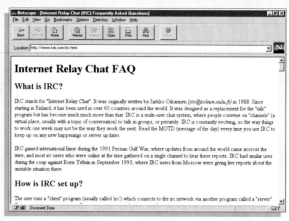

1 The best place to start is the Internet Relay Chat FAQ (frequently asked questions) page on the Web. Type the following URL into your browser's location entry box and press Enter: **http://www.kei.com/irc.html**. For those new to IRC, the information at the top of the page is an excellent summary of what IRC is and how it works.

9 You can leave the current channel by closing the window. You can also open an additional channel by selecting it from the Channels folder. In fact, you can have multiple channels open at the same time, and you can switch between them as often as you like.

Chat window   **Active participants list**

8 Now you're actively participating in an IRC session. The main chat window is divided into two panes. The left side of the window displays all the messages left by users on the channel. The right side of the window maintains a running list of all the participants in the channel. You can type a message and press Enter to broadcast it.

TIP SHEET

▶ **IRC has its own culture and rules of etiquette, often referred to as "netiquette." To avoid getting "flamed," or assaulted by e-mail for breaching the accepted rules of IRC, be sure to take a few minutes to read through the IRC FAQ. It will answer most of the basic questions you'll have about IRC. You can also ask questions in the #newbies channel.**

▶ **Netscape users can download a special chat program called Netscape Chat. It is designed to work with the Netscape Navigator Web browser. You can download it for free from Netscape's home page at http://home.netscape.com.**

2 The most crucial piece of the IRC puzzle is an IRC client application. This is the software program that will allow you to connect to and participate in an IRC session. The IRC FAQ contains a section with hyperlinks to FTP sites that carry downloadable IRC client applications. Scroll through the FAQ until you reach this section and click on any link to open the FTP site of your choice.

3 One of the most popular IRC client applications is mIRC, a freeware program for Windows. You can download the latest version from the mIRC home page at http://www.sbcomp.com/mirc/index.html.

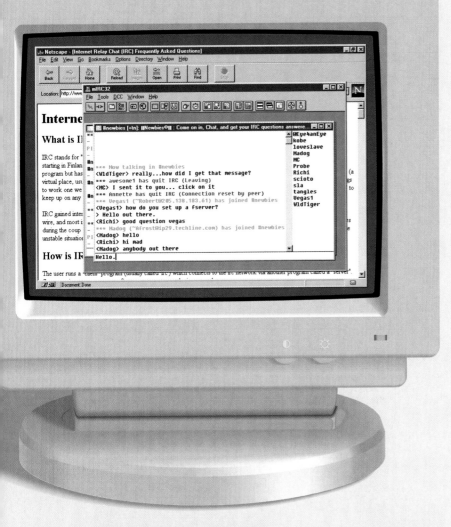

4 After you have downloaded and installed mIRC, launch the program. The first thing you'll need to do is to enter some setup information. Choose Setup from the File menu, or press Ctrl+E.

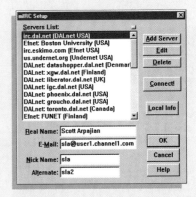

5 In the mIRC setup screen, choose a server from the server list. Then type in your real name and your e-mail address in the text entry boxes provided. You must also provide a nickname, which will be used to identify you on the IRC channels. You should also enter an alternate nickname, in case your first choice is already in use.

7 Click on the channels folder on the mIRC toolbar. This will bring up a list of available channels. For starters, join a new users channel, such as #newbies. Click on either the Join or OK button once you have selected a channel.

6 Press the Connect button to log on to the IRC server.

How to Use Multiuser Games on the Internet

Gaming on the Internet is very popular, especially in the form of Multiuser Dungeons (MUDs). MUDs aren't necessarily dark and scary, but they can be addictive, and it's easy to get trapped inside. A MUD is an interactive game in which you assume the identity of a character and play against other characters who are also online. MUDs come in many different shapes and sizes, but all of them share one thing in common—they're a lot of fun. This section will point you to some MUD resources as well as some other popular Web sites for games and gaming.

1 MUDs are not actually part of the World Wide Web. They are accessed through a Telnet connection using a Telnet client application. While any Telnet application will do, using a specialized MUD client program is an even better choice. A good place to start your search for a MUD client is the Winsock Game Clients page at http://www.rahul.net/galen/client.html. This page contains information and links to many popular MUD programs, and even has a chart comparing their features.

6 MUDs may be the most popular form of gaming on the Internet, but they're not the only games available. There is a growing number of Web-based games appearing, and there are several resources avaiable to help you find them. One of these is the Games Domain at http:// www.gamesdomain.co.uk.

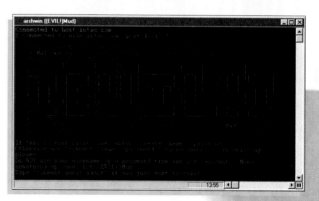

5 Once you've connected to a MUD, follow the directions on the screen carefully. Getting used to the world of MUDs takes a little time. It's a good idea to type **help** at the prompt to get specific information on commands you can use in the MUD. For general help with MUDs, you can access the MUD Resource Collection page at http://www.cis.upenn.edu/~lwl/ mudinfo.html.

TIP SHEET

▶ **MUD is often used as a catch-all term for any role-playing game on the Internet, but there are lots of different varieties. Object-oriented MUDs are called MOOs, and MUSHs are Multiuser Shared Hallucinations.**

▶ **Currently most online games are text based, but as the technology develops and better ways of handling multimedia on the Web become widespread, the gaming environment will soon become fully visual and auditory. Watch for graphical multiuser games to continue to grow in popularity in the months to come.**

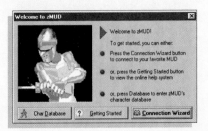

2 One of the best MUD client programs is Zugg's MUD Client (zMUD), which can be downloaded from the zMUD home page at http://www.rt66.com/~zugg/zmud.htm. This full-featured MUD client boasts a Connection Wizard that makes accessing MUDs a snap.

3 Once you've downloaded and installed your MUD client, you need to find a MUD game to join. Most client programs come with a list of available MUDs, but you can find a current and comprehensive list on the Web at the Mud Connector Web page. The URL is http://www.absi.com/mud-bin/mud_biglist.cgi.

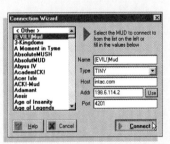

4 Now that you have a MUD client and a list of active MUDs that you can join, it's time to jump right in. Using the instructions provided by your MUD client, connect to a MUD. If you're using zMUD, click on the Connection Wizard button when you start the program, or choose Connection Wizard from the File menu. Select the MUD you wish to join and press the Connect button.

CHAPTER 9

The Evolving Web: Java

 The hottest buzzword on the Internet these days is *Java*. You may have heard about it while browsing the Web, or you may have seen it screaming at you from the cover of a computing magazine. Java is the most exciting thing to happen to the World Wide Web since the Web itself.

What is Java? It is a programming language for the World Wide Web, developed by Sun Microsystems. Although the thought of another computer programming language doesn't necessarily stir the souls of most normal people, Java is exciting because of what it means for the Web.

Web sites can now be truly interactive. Java-enabled browsers such as Netscape can download Java programs, called *applets*, and execute them inside the browser window, where they appear to be part of the Web page. This allows users to actually do something on the page, rather than simply look at it.

Understanding Java

There's a lot of hype surrounding Java, which means that its capabilities and limitations are easily misunderstood. In this section, you'll learn a little about the basics of Java.

▶ ❶ Java was developed by software engineers at Sun Microsystems. The Java home page is at http://java.sun.com. The home page contains many useful links for learning about Java or for getting a start in programming your own Java applets.

TIP SHEET

▶ If you're interested in tinkering with Java, one of the best ways to learn about the language is to look at applet source code. Many Java programmers release their source code and make it available for downloading along with the applet. Sun Microsystems also maintains an applets page with plenty of Java source code at http://java.sun.com/applets/index.html.

❻ Java is a secure programming language. Before each Java program is run, it is first checked by the browser to ensure that it is a valid Java application. This makes it difficult for a computer virus to be transported inside a Java applet.

2 Java is a simple programming language, based on C++, but much less complicated. The Java Development Kit is available for free, and can be downloaded from http://java.sun.com/JDK-1.0/index.html.

3 Java is an object-oriented language. This means that most of the material in one Java applet can be reused in another. The result is that development in Java is easier and takes less time than in many traditional programming languages. New Java applets, partially based on existing ones, are being released every day.

4 Java applets are downloaded and executed on the client machine instead of the Web server. This reduces server traffic and improves performance. Java applets are also small and can be downloaded quickly, making them ideal for use on the Web.

5 Java is a platform-independent language. That means that the same Java application can run on different computer systems. There's no need for Java developers to create and test different programs for PCs, Macintosh, and UNIX systems.

What Can You Do with Java?

Java is exciting from a technological stand-point, but what really makes Java cool is what it can do. There are thousands of Java applets available on the Web, and simply browsing around can give you an idea of what can be done with Java. Here are a few examples of what's already being done with this versatile programming language.

 1 Java can be used to create animation. This is quickly becoming the most common use for Java applets. In most cases, animation is used to add visual appeal to Web sites. However, there are practical uses for animation as well.

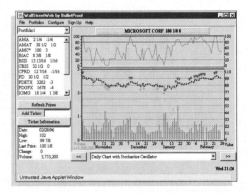

7 Java can also be used to develop complex applications on the Web, such as this stock tracking program, which retrieves stock quotes periodically from a server and displays stock ticker and graph information in a window. The applet can be customized, and individual preferences can be set using the program's menus.

TIP SHEET

▶ To keep on top of what's really cool in the world of Java, create a bookmark for the Gamelan What's Cool page. This site tracks the most exciting and innovative Java applets, and updates the list several times each week. The Gamelan What's Cool page can be found at http://www.gamelan.com/.

▶ Another site that tracks the top Java applets is JARS (Java Applet Rating Service). JARS rates applets in several categories and publishes the results on its home page at http://www.jars.com.

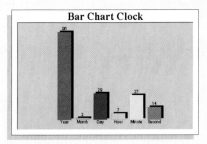

2 News tickers are another popular use for Java. These are typically used to scroll news headlines across a Web page, and are able to convey a lot of information without forcing the reader to scroll through the page. Java allows each item to become a hyperlink to a different page. When the user clicks on a particular head-line, the applet will instruct the Web browser to load a new page with the full news story.

3 Java applets can be used to display dynamic charts and graphs, which can instantly update the display as new information is received.

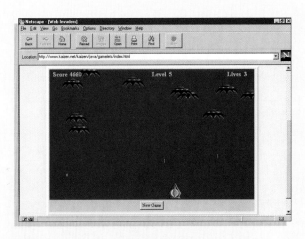

4 Java can be used to create clickable graphics with "live feedback." There are already many clickable image maps on the Web, which send users to different Web sites depending on where they click. However, Java allows Web design-ers to give visual clues with the images. In this example, the button turns green as it is pressed.

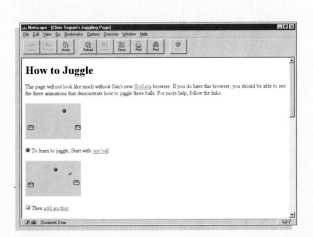

5 Java can be used to create interactive games on the Web. Java's graphics and animation capabilities bring whole new possibilities for gaming on the Internet.

6 Java can be used to create educational sites on the Web. Java allows real-time feedback, making it ideal for simple educational games and tutorials.

How to Learn More about Java on the Web

If you're interested in learning more about Java, the best place to turn is the Web itself. There are several Java resources on the Web, and as the language becomes more popular, a growing number of sites for Java enthusiasts are appearing.

1 The first place to look for information about Java is Sun Microsystems's Java home page. Point your browser to http://java.sun.com.

5 If you're interested in more advanced Java programming, take a look at the Java Developer home page at http://www.digitalfoucus.com/digitalfocus/faq/. It contains lists of Java resources, a Job Forum, and information on retail Java tools and add-ons.

TIP SHEET

▸ You can also find out more about Java in the Usenet newsgroup comp.lang.java. This newsgroup has frequent postings about Java programming, tips, and techniques.

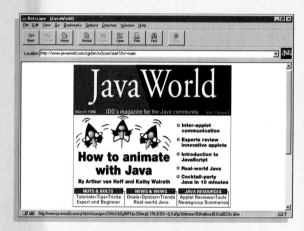

2 Gamelan is a comprehensive repository of Java applets. If you're looking for a particular type of applet, look here first. The site is organized into categories, and features a search engine to help you find exactly what you're looking for. You can visit the Gamelan site by pointing your browser to http://www.gamelan.com.

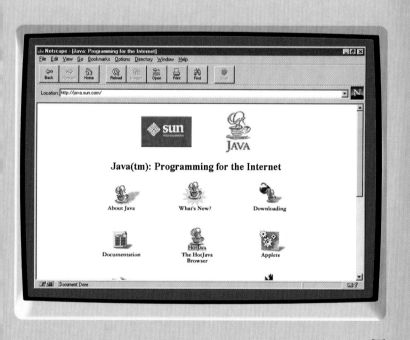

3 JavaWorld magazine contains tips, tricks, and suggestions for programming in Java. It also has regular features and interviews with the Java professionals. You can visit JavaWorld's home page on the Web at http://www.javaworld.com/.

4 If you want to learn how to program in Java, you should visit the *Brewing Java: a Tutorial* page on the Web at http://sunsite.unc.edu/javafaq/ javatutorial.html. This site has an extensive guide to the Java language and compiler and is geared toward the beginning Java programmer.

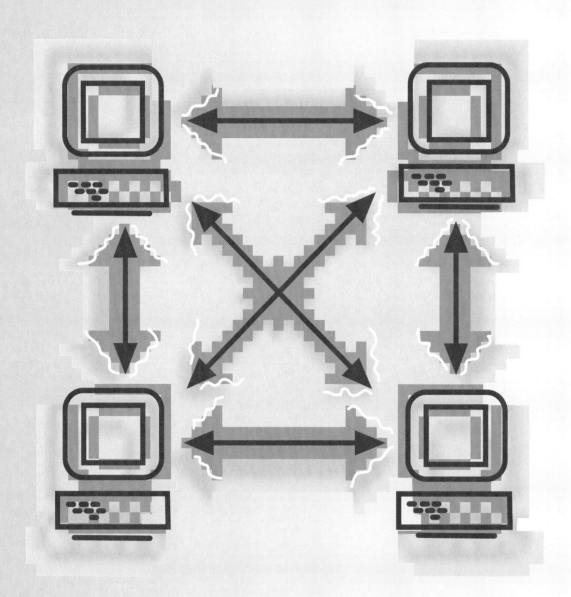

CHAPTER 10

The Evolving Web: Virtual Reality with VRML

 We live in a three-dimensional world. As exciting as browsing the Web can be, today's Web pages are limited to two dimensions. All things considered, browsing the Web is little more than reading a sophisticated electronic newspaper.

The developers of VRML, which is short for *Virtual Reality Modeling Language*, want to change that. VRML allows for the creation of simulated 3-D worlds in which you browse interactively. You can explore, hyperlink to other VRML worlds or other parts of the Internet, and even chat with other users.

VRML works in much the same way as "normal" HTML Web pages. Like HTML, VRML worlds are encoded in a language that is interpreted by a special browser on the end user's machine. The VRML browser does most of the work involved with rendering and displaying the actual graphics. This saves a tremendous amount of time, because once the VRML world information has been downloaded, it doesn't need to be re-sent each time the user moves around.

In this chapter, you'll learn about the basics of VRML, as well as how to download and use a VRML browser. VRML is a new and exciting direction for the Web, and after you finish this chapter, you'll be ready to jump right in.

Understanding VRML

VRML is a fascinating new concept for the Internet, and it is becoming increasingly popular as technological advances in graphics hardware and 3-D software tools progress. In the meantime, understanding the concept of VRML and how it works is still difficult for many. In this section, you'll get a brief glimpse of what VRML is and what it can do, as well as how to find out more information about exploring and creating your own VRML worlds.

▶ **1** VRML is a language for describing 3-D objects, and is used primarily to create simulated 3-D worlds on the World Wide Web.

5 VRML can be combined with Java to create interactive 3-D games on the Web. For example, VRML Fighter simulates combat between two opponents in a VRML world. To see VRML Fighter in action, visit the site at http://www. netscape.com/comprod/products/ navigator/live3d/examples/fighter/ fghtentr.html. You will need Netscape 2.0 with Netscape's Live3D VRML browser.

TIP SHEET

▶ **You can find out even more about VRML, including the official VRML specification, at the VRML Repository. The URL for the VRML Repository is http://www.sdsc.edu/0/SDSC/ Partners/vrml/.**

▶ **Many VRML worlds contain hyperlinks to other VRML worlds, or even to other items on the Web, such as Web pages or FTP sites. When your mouse cursor passes over a hyperlink in a VRML world, it will usually change from the standard pointer to a hand. Most VRML browsers also display a description of the hyperlink on screen when the mouse cursor passes over it. To follow a link, simply click on it.**

2 Users explore VRML worlds with a VRML browser. This can be a separate program, or it can be an add-on or plug-in to an existing Web browser, such as Netscape or Internet Explorer.

3 You can navigate in a 3-D VRML world with either a keyboard, a mouse, or a combination of both. Most VRML browsers offer several different modes of navigation, such as walking or flying.

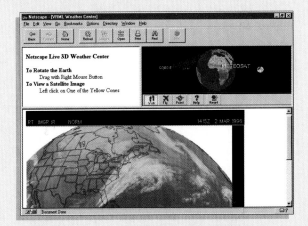

4 Although many VRML worlds are fictional, VRML technology can be used for many practical purposes, such as the VRML Weather Center, which allows you to view several different satellite images of the Earth. By rotating the 3-D model of Earth, you can choose a particular satellite view.

How to Use VRML with Live3D

Netscape's Live3D is a VRML add-on for the Netscape Navigator Web browser. It plugs directly into the browser, so VRML worlds can appear to be part of a Web page. The Live3D browser is available for free from Netscape, and makes exploring VRML worlds easy and fun.

1 You can download the Live 3D browser from Netscape's Live3D Home page at http://www.netscape.com/comprod/products/navigator/live3d/index.html.

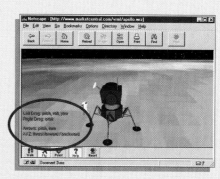

7 If you click on the Help button in the toolbar, Live3D will display brief navigational directions in the lower left-hand corner of the screen.

TIP SHEET

▶ **If you become hopelessly lost in a VRML world, just click on the Reset button in the Live3D toolbar. It will take you back to the place where you started browsing.**

2 Once you have run the Live3D installation program, you will be able to view VRML worlds. Netscape will recognize a VRML world and launch Live3D automatically.

3 Live3D's simple toolbar gives you all the controls you need for navigating VRML worlds. By default, the VRML browser is in Walk mode, which simulates movement on a flat surface—just like walking on the ground.

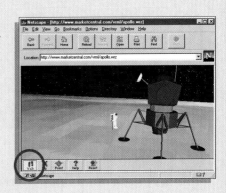

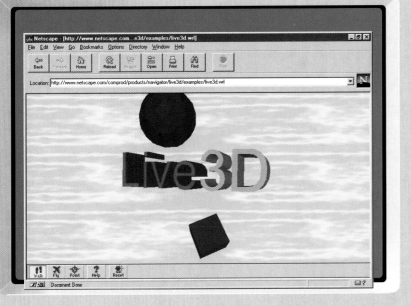

4 To navigate in Walk mode, click the left mouse button and hold it down. Then drag the cursor in the direction you want to move. Dragging the cursor towards the top of the screen moves you forward. Dragging the cursor towards the bottom of the screen moves you backward. Dragging the cursor sideways rotates you in a circle. You can also use the arrow keys on your keyboard to navigate with Live3D.

5 Fly mode simulates free movement in all directions. The controls work like those in an airplane, so clicking and dragging the cursor upward actually sends you in a downward direction, and vice-versa. Clicking and dragging the cursor to either the left or right rotates you in the corresponding direction. You can use the A and Z keys to thrust forward and backward, respectively. Navigating in Fly mode takes a little practice, but once you get the hang of it, you'll be zooming through VRML worlds in no time.

6 In Point mode, double-clicking on an object immediately zooms you in close. You can use Point mode to navigate directly to a particular place in a VRML world. While in point mode, you can use the arrow keys on your keyboard to make minor adjustments to your viewpoint and position.

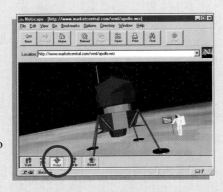

How to Use VRML with Internet Explorer

Microsoft offers a free VRML add-in for use with its Internet Explorer Web browser. The VRML add-in supports all the common VRML navigation functions and is easy to install and use. It is readily available from Microsoft's Web site, and is the perfect VRML solution for Internet Explorer users.

▶ ❶ To download the VRML add-in for Internet Explorer, visit the Internet Explorer home page at http://www. microsoft.com/windows/ie/vrml.htm.

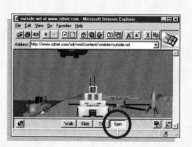

❼ The Spin button allows you to rotate around the center of the VRML world, remaining at a constant distance from the center point. You can spin in a full 360-degree field of motion by clicking and dragging your cursor in the direction that you want to move.

TIP SHEET

▶ The reset button, located on the right side of the toolbar, allows you to return to the starting point of the VRML world. The straighten button, which is located next to the reset button, returns you to your original orientation, although it does not change your actual position in the VRML world.

2 Follow the instructions provided for downloading and installing the VRML add-in. One installed, the VRML add-in will become integrated with Internet Explorer, and you'll automatically be able to browse VRML worlds from within your Web browser.

3 The VRML add-in uses a simple toolbar for navigational controls. You begin in Walk mode, which simulates movement on a flat surface, as if you were walking on the ground.

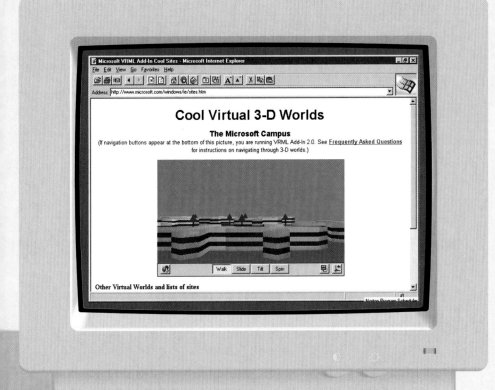

4 To navigate in Walk mode, click the left mouse button and hold it down. Then drag the cursor in the direction you want to move. Dragging the cursor toward the top of the screen moves you forward. Dragging the cursor toward the bottom of the screen moves you backward. Dragging the cursor sideways rotates you in a circle. You can also use the arrow keys on your keyboard to navigate.

5 Slide mode allows you to move either up, down, left, or right without moving forward or backward. To move in Slide mode, click the mouse button and drag the cursor in the direction you want to slide.

6 Clicking on the Tilt button allows you to roll and adjust your pitch. To pitch upwards or downwards, click and drag the mouse cursor up or down, respectively. Dragging the cursor to the left or right causes you to roll in either direction.

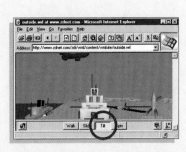

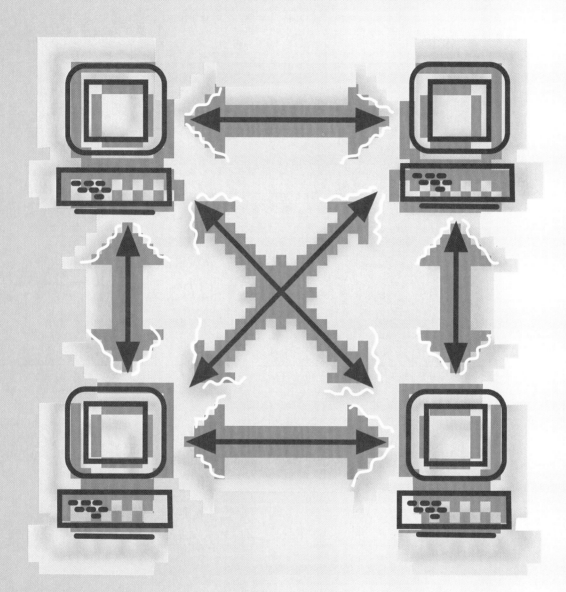

CHAPTER 11

The Evolving Web: Netscape Plug-Ins

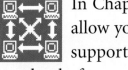 In Chapter 6, you learned about helper applications, which allow you to view file types on the Web that are not directly supported by your browser. Helper applications run independently from your Web browser and display the file contents in a separate window. Plug-ins take the concept one step further—they work seamlessly with Netscape's Navigator to make the file appear as though it's directly part of the Web page you're viewing.

The result is that Web page designers can create pages for Netscape users with rich multimedia and exciting content. Plug-ins benefit the user, because once you install the plug-in, you don't have to do anything else—the plug-in works automatically.

Plug-ins can also be used for much more than spicing up a Web page. In this chapter, you'll learn about plug-ins such as Inso's Word Document Viewer, which allows Netscape users to view Microsoft Word documents on the Web, complete with formatting, even if they do not have Word installed on their system.

Plug-ins are an exciting development, and make browsing the Web with Netscape a much fuller experience.

Understanding Plug-Ins

In this section, you'll learn the basics of plug-ins, including what makes them different from helper applications. You'll also learn about how to download and install plug-ins for use with the Netscape Navigator Web browser.

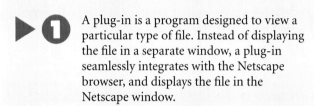

1 A plug-in is a program designed to view a particular type of file. Instead of displaying the file in a separate window, a plug-in seamlessly integrates with the Netscape browser, and displays the file in the Netscape window.

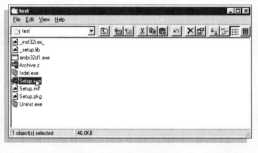

5 Sometimes the plug-in comes packaged as a self-extracting file, which means that double-clicking on it will cause the file to extract all of its individual components, but not start the installation process. If your plug-in is self-extracting, you'll need to wait for it to finish and then double-click on setup.exe or install.exe to begin the installation.

TIP SHEET

▶ Plug-ins work in a similar fashion to helper applications, and rely on MIME types to identify files on the Internet. You can learn more about helper applications by turning back to Chapter 6.

▶ You can learn more about the technical aspects of how plug-ins work by reading Netscape's plug-in development guide. To read the guide, point your Web browser to http://home.netscape.com/eng/mozilla/2.0/handbook/plugins/index.html.

2 Plug-ins work transparently to the user. Once you have installed a plug-in, you don't need to do anything special to activate it. When you access a file type supported by a plug-in, it will be displayed automatically.

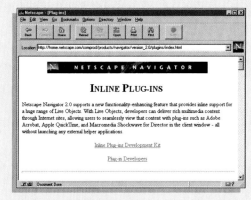

3 A growing number of companies are developing plug-ins for use with Netscape. You can find a list of them on Netscape's Web site. From there, you can find links to download the plug-in files. To access this list, type http://home.netscape.com/comprod/products/navigator/version_2.0/plugins.index.html into your Web browser's location box and press Enter.

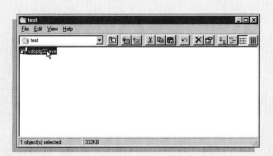

4 Most plug-ins come ready to install after downloading. Usually, they will be packaged in a self-installing executable file. Move the plug-in file to a temporary folder, and double-click on it to begin installation.

How to Use Shockwave

Macromedia's Shockwave plug-in allows Web designers to include Macromedia Director movies in their presentations. Director is an industry-standard multimedia authoring tool, and is used extensively for CD-ROM projects.

Shockwave supports most of the features of full Director movies, including animation, music, and sound effects. Macromedia's Director is famous for making CD-ROMs come to life, and Shockwave does the same for the Web.

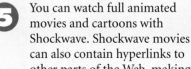

1 The Shockwave plug-in is available for downloading from Macromedia's home page on the Web. Type the URL http://www.macromedia.com/Tools/Shockwave/index.html into your browser's location text box to get there.

5 You can watch full animated movies and cartoons with Shockwave. Shockwave movies can also contain hyperlinks to other parts of the Web, making them truly interactive.

TIP SHEET

▸ There are many examples of Shockwave movies in Macromedia's Shockwave Gallery. To see how Shockwave is being used on the Web, point your Web browser to http://www.macromedia.com/Tools/Shockwave/Gallery/index.html.

▸ If you're interested in finding out how to create your own Shockwave movies with Macromedia's Director, visit the Macromedia Shockwave Developer's Center at http://www.macromedia.com/Tools/Shockwave/sdc/Dev/index.html.

2 Once you've installed the Shockwave plug-in, Netscape will automatically launch the Shockwave player when it encounters Shockwave movies on the Web. Shockwave movies are designed to play inside the Netscape browser window and appear as though they are part of the current Web page.

3 Almost any Macromedia Director movie can be adapted for use with Shockwave. For example, an animated corporate logo can be displayed on a company's home page.

4 Shockwave can also be used to create interactive games, such as this one, which involves throwing darts at balloons. In this example, the user controls the on-screen hand with the mouse, and attempts to pop as many balloons as possible. The direction and speed of the dart are controlled with the mouse. Full sound effects accompany the animation.

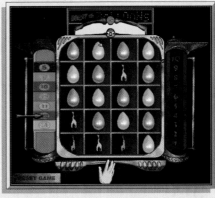

How to Use Adobe's Acrobat Amber Reader

Adobe's Portable Document Format (PDF) is a popular file format for creating electronic documents. All of the text, graphics, and layout information is stored in the PDF file, giving the author precise control over the look and feel of the document. The PDF format is cross-platform, meaning that the same file can be read on PCs and Macintosh computers, as long as they are equipped with a special reader.

Portable Document Format files have become increasingly popular on the Web, because they give designers much more control than standard HTML codes. One limitation of PDF is that a special viewer, the Adobe Acrobat Reader, is required. In the past, this meant that users needed to set up the Acrobat Reader as a helper application, and view PDF files in a separate window. However, the new Adobe Acrobat Amber Plug-in for Netscape makes reading PDF files as simple as browsing the Web.

TIP SHEET

▶ There are many .PDF format files on the Web. Adobe maintains a list of sites using .PDF files at http://w1000.mv. us.adobe.com/Acrobat/PDFsites.html.

▶ You can download official tax forms from the IRS in PDF format by visiting the IRS home page at http://www.irs. ustreas.gov/prod/.

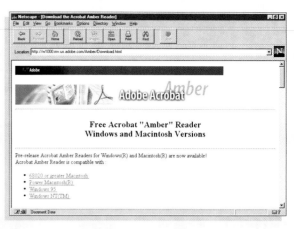

▶ **1** You can download the Adobe Acrobat Amber reader from Adobe's Web site at http://w1000.mv.us.adobe.com/Amber /Download.html.

5 You can print the PDF file by choosing Print from Netscape's File menu.

2 The Amber reader features a simple toolbar for common functions, such as navigating through the pages in a document. Moving from page to page is simple with familiar "VCR style" controls. You can click on the forward or backward arrows to move one page at a time. You can also jump immediately to the first or last page in a document. The double arrow icons allow you to move backward and forward through the sequence of pages that you have read, which may not be the same as the actual page order.

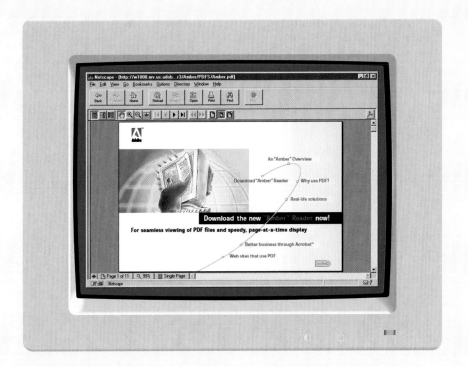

3 You can change your view of the document with the page size buttons on the toolbar. You can choose between normal (100%) view, close-up (124%) view, and a special view that fits the entire page inside the current window.

4 You can also use the magnification buttons to zoom in and out of a particular portion of the page. For example, to zoom in, click on the button with a plus sign, and then click on the area of the document that you want to magnify.

How to Use RealAudio

RealAudio, from Progressive Networks, allows you to listen to live audio feeds over the Internet. The technology has become very popular on the Web, and several companies are already providing regular programming with RealAudio.

Originally, RealAudio was available only as a separate helper application, but now it can also be used as a plug-in for Netscape. With RealAudio running in the background, you can see and hear the Web all at once.

▶ ❶ You can download the RealAudio player from the RealAudio home-page at http://www.realaudio.com.

TIP SHEET

▶ **You can visit many Web sites using RealAudio v2.0. To see a list, point your Web browser to http://www. realaudio.com/products/ra2.0/sites/.**

▶ **You can find out how to incorporate RealAudio files as plug-ins in your own pages by visiting this URL: http://www.realaudio.com/products/ ra2.0/plug_ins/index.html. For more information on creating your own Web pages, see Chapter 12.**

2 The RealAudio Player works both as a helper application and as a plug-in. Once the RealAudio player is installed, Netscape will automatically launch whichever version of RealAudio it needs, which is determined by the Web page designer.

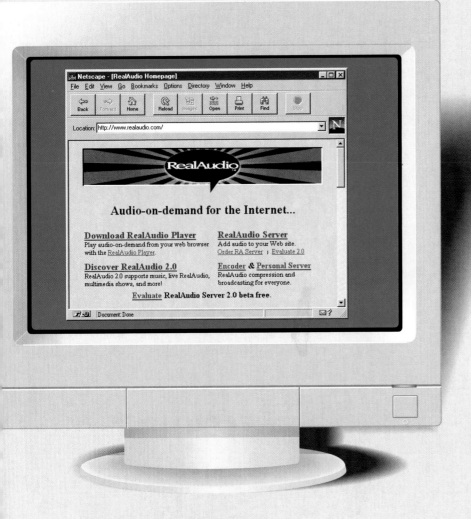

3 When the RealAudio player is used as a plug-in, the player and controls appear to be embedded in the actual Web page. You can view information about the file currently playing, as well as adjust the volume and pause or stop the playback.

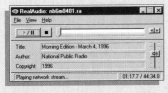

4 When the RealAudio Player is launched as a helper application, it appears in a separate window. A full range of features is available, including volume and playback controls.

How to Use Inso's Word Viewer Plug-In

Inso Corporation's Word Viewer Plug-in lets you view Microsoft Word 6.0 and 7.0 documents with Netscape 2.0. The Word documents can be viewed even if the end users do not have Microsoft Word installed on their systems. Word documents can be viewed in full-screen mode or embedded within a Web page.

All of the fonts, formatting, tables, and graphics from the original Word document are preserved by the plug-in viewer.

▶ **1** You can download the Word Viewer Plug-in from the Inso home page at http://www.inso.com/plug.htm.

6 You can also select objects from inside the Word document and copy them to the clipboard. First, select the items and then right-click. Then, choose Copy from the menu.

TIP SHEET

▶ **The Word Viewer plug-in is ideal for companies that have existing documents in Word format and want to publish them on the Web with full formatting and graphics intact.**

▶ **You can see examples of Word documents embedded in Web pages by visiting the Inso Corporation home page at http://www.inso.com/plugsamp.htm.**

2 Once the Word Viewer Plug-in is installed, Netscape will automatically launch the Word Viewer whenever a Word document is encountered on the Web. If the Web designer has embedded the Word document inside the page, the Word document will appear inside the main Netscape window.

3 You can scroll through an embedded Word document using the scroll bars.

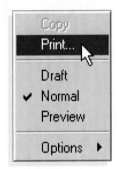

4 To print the Word document, place the cursor over it and right-click. Then choose Print from the menu.

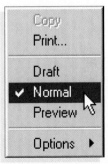

5 You can change the view of the Word document to either Normal, Draft, or Print Preview by choosing the appropriate selection from the same menu.

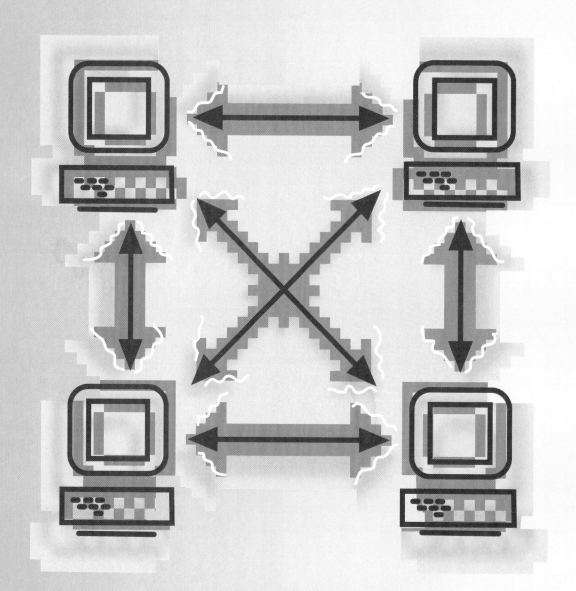

CHAPTER 12

Creating and Launching Your Own Web Page

 Now that you've seen all the cool stuff you can do with a Web page, you may be curious about getting out there with your own personal message for the world. Fortunately, publishing on the Web is easy.

The language of the Web is HTML, which is short for *Hypertext Markup Language.* HTML is used to describe the contents of a Web page and how it should look. Web browsers read HTML documents, and then display them according to the layout instructions contained in the HTML codes. Fortunately, HTML is very simple to understand and use, and it only requires knowledge of a few simple commands.

This chapter will briefly discuss some of the fundamentals of Web page publishing, starting with the basics of HTML. You'll also learn how to use a full-featured Web page creation tool, Netscape Gold. Finally, you'll discover how easy it is to publish your own home page on the Web through the major online services, America Online, Compu-Serve, and Prodigy.

How to Create a Simple Web Page

Web pages are created using HTML, the Hypertext Markup Language. HTML is a language that describes how a document should look when viewed with a Web browser. It is not a programming language, and the markup tags used in HTML are very simple and easy to understand. HTML is written in plain ASCII text, and HTML documents can be created with just about any word processor or text editor, including the very basic editor, Windows Notepad.

In this section, you'll learn how to create a very simple Web page using Notepad in Windows 95.

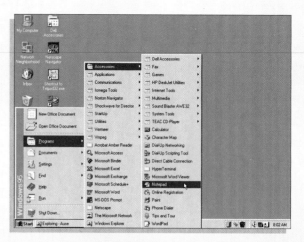

1 Launch Notepad by selecting it from the Accessories folder in the Windows Start menu.

```
<BODY>
<H1>My First Web Page</H1>

<P>Welcome to my very first Web page. I never
realized that creating a Web page in HTML could
be so simple.</P>
|
```

8 Most text in Web pages is grouped together in paragraphs. Paragraphs are enclosed with a <P> and </P> tag pair. These tags let the Web browser know to start a new paragraph. Most Web browsers will insert a blank line and indent the start of each new paragraph. Type in the first paragraph for your HTML document as shown. (*Continued on next page.*)

```
<BODY>
<H1>My First Web Page</H1>
|
```

7 The first element to place in your HTML document is a headline. Generally, the top headline for your Web page should be the title of the page. Headlines are marked using the <H1> and </H1> tag pair. You can adjust the size of the headline by changing the number following the *H* inside both tags. The headline size can range from 1 to 6; the higher the number, the smaller the headline type size. Type <H1>**My First Web Page**</H1> and press Enter.

2 Type <**HTML**> and press Enter. This is the <HTML> tag, which tells the Web browser that the document it is reading is an HTML document. All tags written in HTML are surrounded by less-than and greater-than angle brackets. The Web browsers read and process HTML tags, but do not display them on screen.

3 Type <**HEAD**> and then press Enter. This is the <HEAD> tag, which marks the beginning of the head section of the HTML document. The head contains basic information about the HTML document, including the document title.

4 Type <**TITLE**>**My First Web Page**</**TITLE**> and press Enter. You just typed in the title of your Web page. The <TITLE> tag specifies the title of the page, which is usually displayed in the title bar of the browser window. Notice the ending </TITLE> tag, which marks the finishing point of the title. Many HTML tags come in pairs, with both a starting and an ending tag. The slash mark inside the tag indicates that it is an ending tag. The Web browser will recognize that the text that falls between these tags is the title of your HTML document.

6 Type <**BODY**> and press Enter. This tag marks the beginning of the body section of your HTML document. The body section contains most of the actual contents of your Web page, including all of the text, graphics, and HTML formatting tags.

5 Type </**HEAD**> to mark the end of the head section and press Enter.

How to Create a Simple Web Page (Continued)

```
<P>Welcome to my very first Web page. I never
realized that creating a Web page in HTML could
be so simple.</P>
<HR>
|
```

▶ **9** Horizontal rules are used in Web pages to mark different sections of the document. Web browsers typically display a thin horizontal line that runs across the width of the page. To insert a horizontal rule in your Web page, type <HR> and press Enter. The <HR> tag is an empty tag, which means that there is no ending </HR> tag.

16 Your Web browser will now display your HTML document. Congratulations! You've just taken the first step toward publishing on the Web.

15 Launch your Web browser and choose Open File from the browser's main menu. Then select myfirst.html, and click on the Open button.

TIP SHEET

▶ Web browsers ignore extra spaces and carriage returns in HTML documents. You should use <P> and </P> tags to separate paragraphs. Don't rely on the formatting you place in your text file.

▶ You can learn much more about creating HTML pages in the book *How to Use HTML3*, from Ziff-Davis Press.

10 To insert an image in your Web document, use the <IMG> tag. Like the <HR> tag, the <IMG> tag is empty and does not have a corresponding ending </IMG> tag. The <IMG> tag also uses attributes, which are placed inside the tag, to give the Web browser information about the image to display. The most important attribute is SRC, which provides the URL of the image.

```
<HR>
<IMG SRC="earth.gif">
|
```

11 Type <**IMG SRC="earth.gif"**> and press Enter. This will instruct the Web browser to display the file earth.gif, which can be found in the same directory as the HTML document. If your image file was located somewhere else, you would type the full URL of the image inside the quotation marks. Since you probably do not have a file named earth.gif on your computer system, feel free to substitute with a different image.

```
Untitled - Notepad
File  Edit  Search  Help
<HTML>
<HEAD>
<TITLE>My First Web Page</TITLE>
</HEAD>
<BODY>
<H1>My First Web Page</H1>

<P>Welcome to my very first Web page. I never
realized that creating a Web page in HTML could
be so simple.</P>
<HR>
<IMG SRC="earth.gif">
</BODY>
</HTML>|
```

```
<HR>
<IMG SRC="earth.gif">
</BODY>
|
```

12 Type </**BODY**> and press Enter to mark the end of the body section.

```
<HR>
<IMG SRC="earth.gif">
</BODY>
</HTML>|
```

13 Type </**HTML**> to mark the end of the HTML document.

14 Save your document in Notepad as **myfirst.html**. HTML files need to have either an .HTM or .HTML extension to be recognized properly by a Web browser.

How to Add Hyperlinks to Your Web Page

Hyperlinks represent the real power of HTML and the Web. You can create links from your Web page to any other element on the Internet. You can link to other pages you've created, or pages published by others. Embedding hyperlinks in your Web pages is a simple process, and can be done by adding one simple tag to your HTML document.

1 Launch Notepad and open the HTML document that you created in the previous section.

8 Launch your Web browser and choose Open File from the browser's main menu. Then select myfirst.html, and click on the Open button. Notice that the hypertext link you created appears next to the image. Clicking on this text will activate the link.

7 Save your document in Notepad by choosing Save from the File menu.

TIP SHEET

▶ **Hyperlinks rely on URLs, which are specific addresses for items on the Internet. For more information on URLs, refer back to Chapter 3, "Web Navigation 101."**

▶ **When you create a hyperlink to another page on the Web, be sure to check the link periodically to make sure it still works. Unfortunately, the URL of the page you link to is not under your control, and it can change at any time.**

▶ **If you leave your Web browser open with your page loaded while you're making changes to the HTML document, remember to reload your page using the Reload button on the toolbar. Your Web browser stores each page in a special memory cache and won't notice the changes you've made until you reload the page.**

```
<IMG SRC="earth.gif">
|
</BODY>
```

2 Insert a blank line in between the <IMG> tag and the </BODY> tag.

```
<IMG SRC="earth.gif">
<A>|
</BODY>
```

3 Type <A> to insert an anchor tag. The anchor tag is used to indicate a hypertext link.

The HREF attribute is placed inside the <A> tag.

```
<IMG SRC="earth.gif">
<A HREF="http://www.nasa.gov">|
</BODY>
```

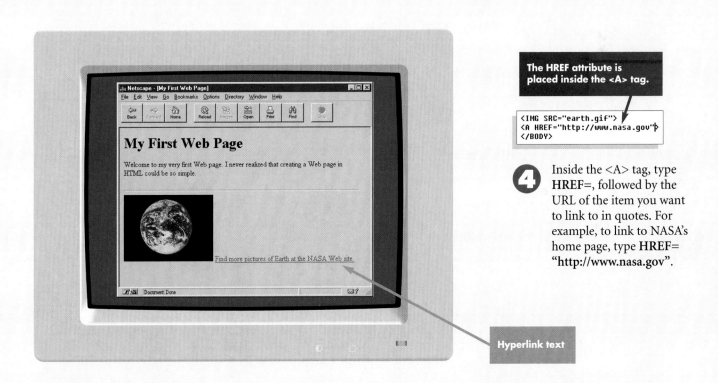

4 Inside the <A> tag, type **HREF=**, followed by the URL of the item you want to link to in quotes. For example, to link to NASA's home page, type **HREF= "http://www.nasa.gov"**.

My First Web Page

Welcome to my very first Web page. I never realized that creating a Web page in HTML could be so simple.

Find more pictures of Earth at the NASA Web site.

Hyperlink text

```
<IMG SRC="earth.gif">
<A HREF="http://www.nasa.gov">Find more pictures
of Earth at the NASA Web site.|
</BODY>
```

5 Next, place the cursor outside of the <A> tag, and type **Find more pictures of Earth at the NASA Web site**. This is the descriptive hypertext that will appear in blue on your Web page. When readers click on this text, the hyperlink will activate and take them to the NASA site.

```
<A HREF="http://www.nasa.gov">Find more pictures
of Earth at the NASA Web site.</A>|
```

6 Type </A> to close the anchor.

How to Place Your Page on the Web

S o far, your "Web" page has really only been an HTML document on your local hard drive. In this section, you'll learn a few basic guidelines for placing your page on the actual World Wide Web, where it can be accessed by anyone with a Web browser.

Unfortunately, there is no one simple way of posting a Web page. The procedures differ, depending on your Internet Service Provider's system and configuration. This section offers only basic guidelines. You should check with your ISP for exact instructions.

If you are using one of the large commercial online services for Web access, refer to the sections that follow for specific instructions on creating and posting Web pages.

▶ **1** Connect to the Internet through your ISP as usual.

7 Once your HTML document and associated files are placed on your ISP's system, you should test them to make sure they work the way you planned. Test the pages with your Web browser to make sure everything is in order.

TIP SHEET

▸ **Depending on your ISP's system configuration, you may need to set file permissions for your HTML documents and associated files. Most UNIX systems, which are widely used as Web servers, use access permission levels for files. You may need to make sure that your files can be read by anyone who wants to visit your Web site. Check with your ISP to see if you need to set access permissions and how it should be done.**

2 To transfer files from your computer system to your ISP, you'll need an FTP transfer client program. This type of program acts like a File Manager, but is specialized for transferring files via the Internet's FTP protocol. One of the best FTP applications available is WS_FTP. You can download the latest version from http://www.csra.net/junodj/ ws_ftp32.htm.

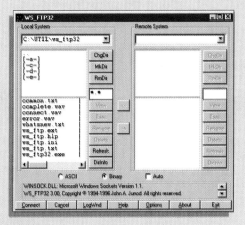

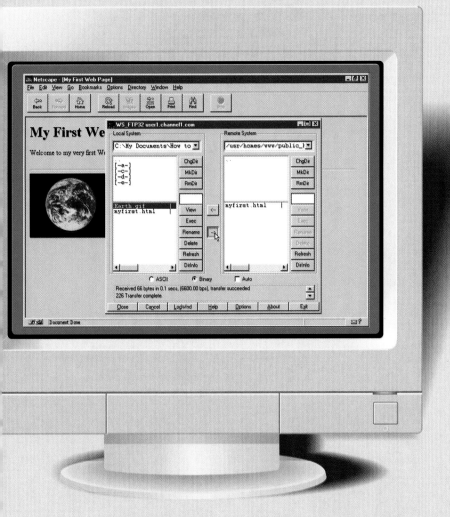

3 Launch your FTP client application.

4 Using your FTP client, establish a connection to your ISP. You'll need to contact your ISP for configuration details beforehand.

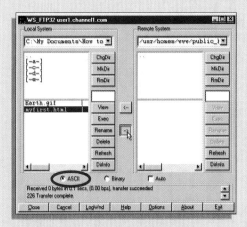

6 If you have any GIF images, sound clips, or other files associated with your HTML document, you should transfer these to your ISP's system in binary mode.

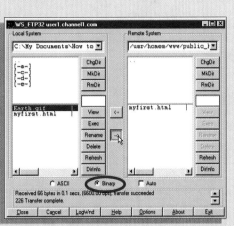

5 The next step is to transfer your HTML document to your ISP's system. FTP client programs support two types of file transfer: ASCII and binary. HTML documents are plain ASCII text files, and need to be transferred in ASCII mode.

How to Create Web Pages on America Online

With over 5 million members, America Online is currently the largest of the commercial online services. One of the reasons for AOL's success is that they have been quick to respond to consumer demand for access to the Internet. In addition to Internet connectivity, AOL offers space on their servers for subscribers to place their own Web pages on the Web. In this section, you'll get a very brief look at the process behind creating and launching a Web page on AOL.

1 Sign on to AOL and then go to the Web Page Toolkit by typing in the keyword **HTML**.

5 Once you're familiar with the process behind uploading files to AOL's server, click on the Go To My Place button to activate the members.aol.com window. This window allows you to transfer files from your computer to AOL's system. After transferring the files, your Web page will be live on the Web.

TIP SHEET

▸ **AOL provides access to help files and tutorials to aid in the process of creating and editing your Web pages and uploading them to the AOL servers. If you have a question about the process, a good way to get your answer is to post it online. The AOL AnswerMan area was set up for just these reasons. To get answers to your questions on Web page publishing, just type in the keyword AnswerMan.**

▸ **You can find home pages of other members on AOL by pointing your Web browser to http://home.aol.com/. Browsing through other member's creations may give you some good ideas for your own Web pages.**

2 AOL has a few options available for Web page publishing. If you would like to use AOL's NaviSoft Software to create your Web page, click on **Go to NaviSoft**. However, assuming you've already created your Web page using the techniques described in the beginning of this chapter, all you need to do is upload your existing Web page to AOL. Click on **Go to Personal Publisher**.

3 From here it is simply a matter of following AOL's on-screen directions. You can go through the AOL tutorial for creating Web pages, search other home pages, or explore other AOL Web page resources. Since you want to publish your own page, double-click on the My Place folder.

4 The next dialog box will prompt you to choose between reading a collection of frequently asked questions and proceeding immediately to the My Place area. Click on the Frequently Asked Questions button for some basic information before proceeding.

How to Create Web Pages on CompuServe

CompuServe has extensive resources for creating and posting your own Web pages. You can create and post your own pages on CompuServe's system using their Home Page Wizard. In this section, you'll take a brief look at the process behind placing Web pages on CompuServe.

 Connect to CompuServe, and then use the GO word **Internet** to access the Internet Center.

TIP SHEET

- ▶ **CompuServe provides access to help files and tutorials to aid in the process of creating and editing your Web pages, as well as loading them on the CompuServe system. For online assistance, click on the Help button, which appears at the bottom of every Home Page Wizard dialog box.**

- ▶ **You can find home pages of other members on CompuServe by visiting CompuServe's OurWorld site at http:// ourworld.compuserve.com/. This site lets you search and browse through other CompuServe subscriber Web pages. It also features a WebMaster's choice of the week, which highlights the best personal pages created by CompuServe members.**

6 Regardless of whether you use the Home Page Wizard or another application to create your Web page, you'll need to use the Publishing Wizard to load you Web pages onto CompuServe's system. Fortunately, the Publishing Wizard is easy to understand, and it automates most of the process. Launch the program and follow the instructions to place your Web pages online.

2 Click on the World Wide Web button. You will be prompted with a dialog box with an option for the CompuServe Home Page Wizard. Double-click on this option.

3 The CompuServe Home Page Wizard is a complete stand-alone application for creating and placing your Web pages on CompuServe's system. It's very simple to use, but also comes with a comprehensive tutorial and online help system. Before using it, you'll need to download the software and install it on your system. Click on the Download the Home Page Wizard! button.

4 Once you have successfully downloaded the software and run the installation program, review the included text files for detailed instructions. The package has two parts: the Home Page Wizard for creating your Web pages, and the Publishing Wizard, which steps you through the process of uploading your pages to CompuServe's system.

5 The Home Page Wizard is very simple and straightforward, although it is not a full-featured HTML editor. If you just want to create a simple Web page with images and hypertext links, however, the Home Page Wizard is an ideal solution. Follow the instructions as you step through the program, and you'll have a working Web page in minutes.

How to Create Web Pages on Prodigy

As with AOL and CompuServe, Prodigy was quick to recognize the growing interest in the Internet, and was actually the first of the three to provide Web access to its members. Now, Prodigy also provides custom Web page publishing capabilities for its members, with all the instructions and software needed. This section will give you a brief introduction to the process behind placing your own Web pages on Prodigy.

▶ **1** Sign on to Prodigy, then go to the Personal Web Pages section. Select JumpTo from the GoTo menu, and type **Personal Web Pages.**

6 The URL for your page will be http:// pages.prodigy.com/, plus your user ID, followed by the file name of your HTML document. For example, if your ID is VMDH31A and the file name is myfirst.htm, the full URL will be http://pages.prodigy.com/VMDH31A/myfirst.htm.

TIP SHEET

▶ **Prodigy maintains a Web site with complete instructions, along with software, image files, and other resources for creating your own Web pages.**

▶ **You can see other pages on the Web created by Prodigy subscribers by pointing your Web browser to http://pages. prodigy.com.**

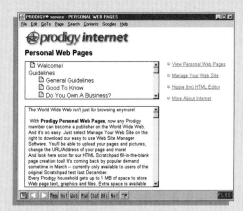

2 You're now at the information menu for creating and launching a Web page via your Prodigy account. Read the Welcome, General Guidelines, and Good To Know files for important information on publishing Web pages on Prodigy.

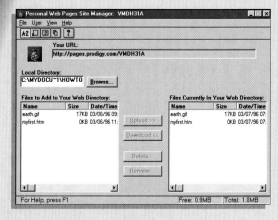

3 Prodigy offers an independent application called the Personal Web Pages Site Manager that works in conjunction with your regular Prodigy software to launch your Web pages on the service. To download this application, click on Manage Your Web Site at the right of the screen.

4 The Personal Web Pages Site Manager has a custom setup and install feature that automatically configures itself on your computer after it is downloaded. It will take you through a brief series of dialog boxes, which allow you to set basic options.

5 Once you have read the instructions and are acquainted with the software, you will use the Personal Web Pages Site Manager to launch your Web pages on Prodigy.

How to Create Web Pages with Netscape Navigator Gold

N etscape Navigator Gold is a new special edition of the popular Netscape Navigator Web browser. The most significant enhancement is its ability to create and edit Web pages Netscape Navigator Gold is a WYSIWYG (What You See Is What You Get) editor, meaning that as you build the page, you'll see what it will look like in its final form.

 You can download the prerelease edition of Netscape Navigator Gold from Netscape's Web site at http://home.netscape.com/com-prod/mirror/index.html.

The editor features a button toolbar that gives you single-click access to many common functions. You can use the button bar to create lists, align text, format text, change the font size, or add additional elements to your page, such as images and hyperlinks. (*Continued on next page.*)

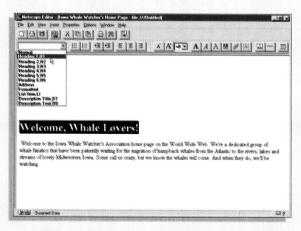

 You can change a portion of the text to a headline. Select the text you'd like to change, and then choose the appropriate Heading value from the drop-down style list box. Headlines range in size from 1 to 6, with size 1 being the largest.

2 To create a new Web page, select New Document from Netscape Navigator Gold's File menu. This will launch the Editing window, where you'll build your page.

3 To enter a title for your Web page, select Document from the Properties menu. A Properties dialog box will appear. Click on the Document Information tab if it is not already selected. Then, type in a title in the text entry box. You can also supply an author name for the document.

Change text colors

Select a background color

Preview your color combinations

Use a background tile image

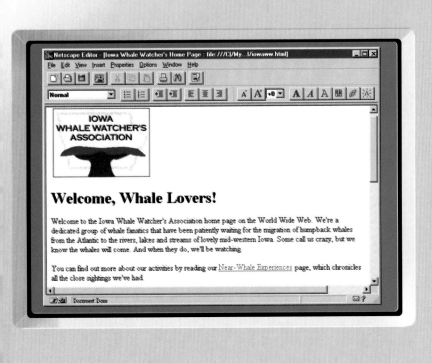

Welcome, Whale Lovers!

Welcome to the Iowa Whale Watcher's Association home page on the World Wide Web. We're a dedicated group of whale fanatics that have been patiently waiting for the migration of humpback whales from the Atlantic to the rivers, lakes and streams of lovely mid-western Iowa. Some call us crazy, but we know the whales will come. And when they do, we'll be watching.

You can find out more about our activities by reading our Near-Whale Experiences page, which chronicles all the close sightings we've had.

4 You can also change the default colors for your Web page by selecting the Colors/Background tab from the Properties dialog box. You can change the colors of normal and hyperlink text. You can also specify a background page color, as well as a background tile image. When you're finished, click on the OK button to return to Netscape Navigator Gold's Editing window.

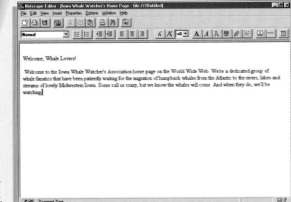

5 To add text to your page, simply begin typing in the edit window.

How to Create Web Pages with Netscape Navigator Gold (Continued)

 To add a list of items to your page, click on either the bulleted or numbered list button in the toolbar. Then type in the items in your list, pressing Enter after each one. When you're finished entering list items, click on the button again.

TIP SHEET

▶ **You can use the Netscape Page Wizard for even easier Web page creation. Using Netscape Navigator Gold, enter the following URL: http:// home.netscape.com/assist/net_sites/ starter/wizard.html. Follow the instructions on screen and within minutes, you'll have a working home page on the Web.**

▶ **Netscape publishes a Navigator Gold Authoring Guide with several tips, tricks, and suggestions for creating Web pages. You can read the guide by pointing your browser to http:// home.netscape.com/eng/ mozilla/ Gold/authoring/navgold.htm.**

 When you're finished creating your Web page, you can upload it to a Web server using Netscape's Navigator Gold's Publish button, or by uploading via FTP using the techniques described earlier in this chapter. Check with your Internet Service Provider to see which method is best for you.

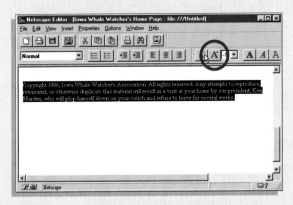

9 You can change the font size of text in your document. First, select the text you'd like to change and then increase or decrease it using the font size buttons on the toolbar.

10 You can also insert a horizontal line anywhere in your document by using the horizontal line button from the toolbar. To change the size and width of the line, right-click on it and choose Horizontal Line Properties from the menu.

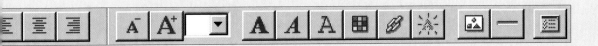

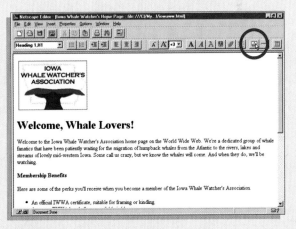

11 You can insert images into your document as well. To insert an image, click on the image icon on the toolbar. The Insert Image dialog box allows you to specify the location of the image and provides a number of formatting options.

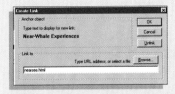

12 Creating hyperlinks with Netscape Navigator Gold is easy. To insert a hyperlink in your document, simply click on the Make Link button in the toolbar. After you specify the text to display for the hyperlink and the URL to link to, your link will be active.

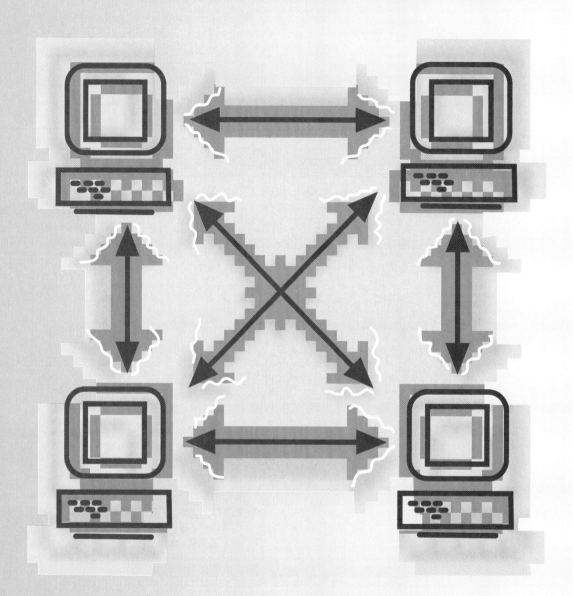

CHAPTER 13

Finding Research and Education Web Sites

 One of first uses of the Web—indeed, one that was a driving force behind its creation—was as a tool for research and education. Someone thought, "Hey, instead of just citing references in footnotes, wouldn't it be better to be able to instantly jump to the work being referenced in a paper with a click of a button?" And so the concept of footnotes was taken to the next level and the hyperlink was born.

In the early days of the Web, only those people in colleges and various private and government research institutes had access to the Web and knew how to use it. Now, of course, the Web has grown to encompass more than just educational use, but this function remains very important. In fact, the largest single group of Web users is still those with an educational focus.

The Web serves educational needs at all levels, from primary and secondary education to special needs education, and from virtual classrooms to vocational training. Professors and students alike are constantly finding new and imaginative ways to use the Web to share ideas and expand access to information. Meanwhile, the technology for delivering multimedia content continues to evolve, allowing educational groups to use the Web to convey ever more captivating and effective institutional materials.

This chapter will introduce a few of the innovative educational institutions that have developed an online Web presence, and show you where to find and share information and educational resources with people around the world.

How to Find Web Sites for Elementary Education

Kids love computers and understand them better than many adults. So it is no wonder that Web sites at elementary schools are popping up all over. The concept of the global community is being strengthened as students at nearly every grade level learn how to communicate and share information with other children in schools located all over the world.

TIP SHEET

▶ **To find schools in your community with a Web page, see the Web66 International School Registry clickable image map at http://web66. coled.umn.edu/schools.html. This site shows a map of the U.S., but has links to maps of Australia, Canada, and Europe as well.**

▶ **Another good web resource for elementary school children is called The Elementary School Student's Internet Gateway and is located at http://volvo.gslis.utexas.edu. It includes Internet do's and don'ts as well as lots of links to kid-specific sites.**

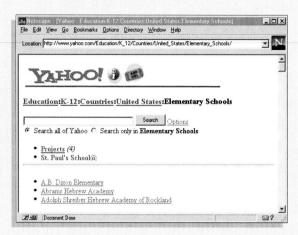

1 At the time of this writing, there are 141 elementary schools listed in Yahoo's search engine. One of Yahoo's fastest growing categories, the elementary schools section was added recently to keep up with the dozens of new listings coming in on a daily basis. Find the Yahoo K-12 listing under the following directory path: Education: K-12: Countries: United_States:Elementary Schools.

5 The Gentle Teaching site at http://www.knoware.nl/users/gentle presents a teaching method developed in the Netherlands for people with learning disabilities and mental retardation. It offers course material and a discussion of the philosophy behind the Gentle Teaching method.

2 Click on Aldershot Elementary School from the Yahoo list, or type the following URL in your browser: http://www.aldershot.nstn.ca/. Mr. Doucet's fifth-grade class at Aldershot Elementary School used their Web page to gather information and pass it along to the attendees of the upcoming G7 summit conference.

3 Type the following URL in your browser's entry window: http://gsn.org/gsn/gsn.home.html. This is a comprehensive Web resource of educational projects developed by and for school children of all ages around the world.

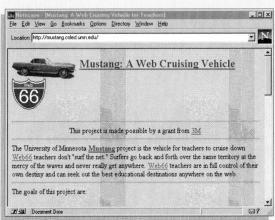

4 The Mustang: A Web Cruising Vehicle site at http://mustang.coled.umn.edu/ has many resources designed specifically to help teachers take control of their Web destiny.

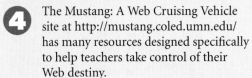

How to Find Web Sites for Secondary Education

E lementary school students aren't the only students on the Web of course. A growing number of secondary educational institutions (grades 7–12) are also getting into the act. As you might expect, these sites often show much more student involvement and a higher level of sophistication.

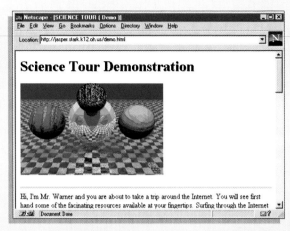

1 Our odyssey begins with a science tour at the Science Tour Demonstration page developed by Dack Warner. Mr. Warner developed this page while teaching science to seventh-grade students in Canton, Ohio. It is a virtual tour through the Internet designed for students at the junior-high school level. The site is at http://jasper.stark.k12.oh.us/demo.html.

TIP SHEET

▶ **The Internet Public Library (IPL) is a virtual library maintained by the University of Michigan that includes online references for youth and classroom education as well as resources for librarians and information professionals. The site is at http://ipl.sils.umich.edu/.**

▶ **To find schools in your community with a Web page, see the Web66 International School Registry clickable image map at http://web66.coled.umn.edu/ schools.html. This site shows a map of the U.S., but has links to maps of Australia, Canada, and Europe as well.**

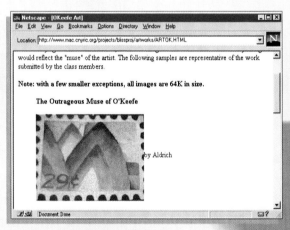

4 Rounding out this section is the Web site created to display the work from a seventh grade language arts project at Cortland Junior-Senior High School. The project involved over 100 students in a collaborative effort containing original student writings and artwork made available in hypermedia form. The results can be seen at http://www.mac.cnyric.org/projects/ blisspro/blisshome.html.

The Issho Kikaku Web site is the home of the SEICHO Project. Based in Japan, this group focuses on youth activity and communications through the Internet to build awareness of environmental problems and solutions. The project home page is at http://www.iac.co.jp/~issho/seicho-conf.html.

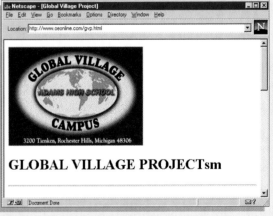

3 The Global Village Project from Adams High School allows students from the senior class to communicate on various project themes with other students around the world. Students use audio, video, fax, and e-mail, and they work collaboratively to develop and complete various projects. The Global Village "campus" is at http://www.oeonline.com/gvp.html.

How to Find Web Resources for Colleges and Universities

Because colleges and universities had some of the first Web sites, the resources available for education at this level are far too numerous to even scratch the surface in one section. The following are a few of the more well-traveled sites, with some suggestions of places to begin exploring online college-level education material.

▶ Because nearly every four-year college or university has some sort of Internet and/or Web presence, there is a good chance you will be able to locate online information about schools all over the world through any of the text-entry search engines. The biggest of these are Yahoo, WebCrawler, Lycos, and InfoSeek. Information about using these search engines can be found in Chapter 7.

▶ **1** One of the best lists of lists for colleges and universities in the U.S. is at Yahoo (again) at http://www.yahoo.com under Education: Universities: United States: Indices. For world-wide indexes follow the path Education: Universities: Indices.

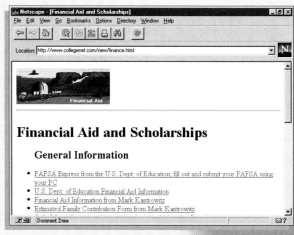

5 And then there's the question of how to pay for college. One handy Web site for people seeking financial aid for college education is the CollegeNet site at http://www.collegenet.com/new/finance.html. Another resource is maintained by Mark Kantrowitz at http://www.cs.cmu.edu/afs/cs.cmu.edu/user/mkant/Public/FinAid/finaid.html.

2 The Yale University Web site has been developed in keeping with the traditions of this university. Tastefully designed, this site focuses on supporting present school activities, but also features alumni resources. The URL is http://www.yale.edu/.

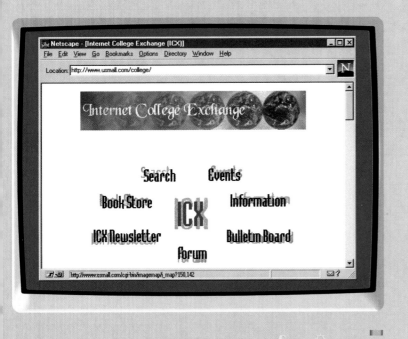

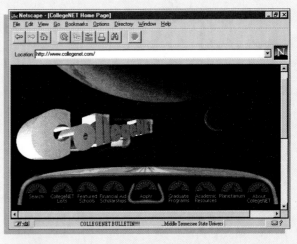

3 A fine list of lists pertaining to admissions information for colleges and universities is maintained by CollegeNet at http://www.collegenet.com/. This well-maintained resource features extensive information on scholarships, and academic resources and listings by geography and area of study.

4 Another good resource for finding the ideal school is the Internet College Exchange at http://www.usmall.com/college/. This site lets you search for the perfect school by comparing your description of the ideal college with all the colleges in the United States.

How to Find General Education Resources on the Web

H ere is a sampling of a few of the more established educational resources on the Web for people of all ages.

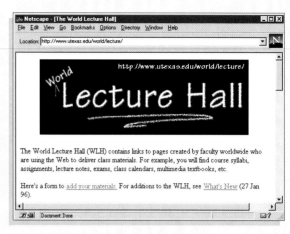

1 Not only is it possible to find extensive information *about* various college and university study programs, you can also find numerous programs at the college level that offer instruction and materials directly online. A good resource for finding online instruction in a variety of course areas is through the World Lecture Hall at http://www.utexas.edu/world/lecture/.

TIP SHEET

▶ **For links to training centers, institutes, and online education resources, see the following Yahoo Education directory: http://www.yahoo.com/Education/. It has extensive lists of links for everything from workplace education to culinary institutes, and resources for educators in both public and private institutions.**

▶ **Another well-organized list of lists is called simply Hotlist and can be found at http://sln.fi.edu/tfi/hotlists/hotlists.html. This is basically a bunch of stuff that educators will find useful, arranged by topic from American History to Wind Energy, and produced by the Franklin Institute.**

5 And last but certainly not least is Uncle Bob's Kids' Page at http://gagme.wwa.com/~boba/kidsi.html. This bright and colorful Web site is known around the world as a virtual treasure chest of links to educational resources for kids, with spotlights on special subjects.

2 The Jason Project should be on every educator's hot list. The site at http://seawifs.gsfc.nasa.gov/scripts/ JASON.html is maintained by NASA and offers an electronic field trip through the Web and around the world.

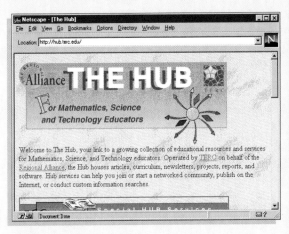

3 Another educational Web site not to be missed is called The Hub and is at http://hub.terc.edu/. This is an "Internetworked" resource for mathematics and science education for students of all ages.

4 The Digital Campus at http://www.linkmag.com/ is a virtual college environment produced by *Link Magazine.* It has everything you might see on a normal college campus, but it only exists in cyberspace. Visit the student union, library, bookstore, or even the local pub for information about beer and coffee, or play a few Internet games to help you relax after class.

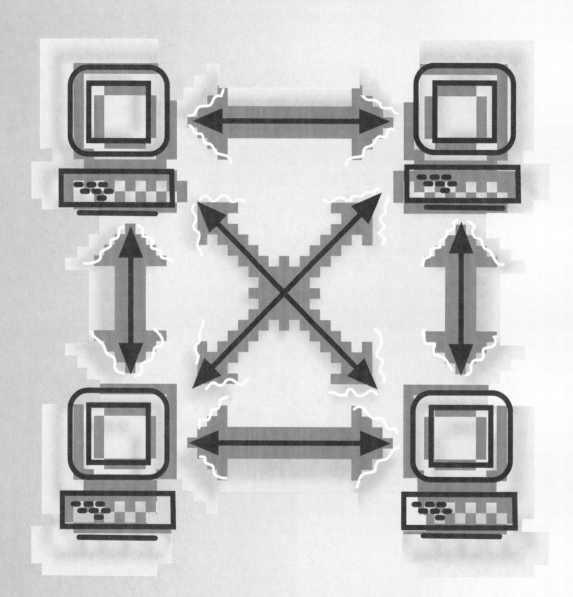

CHAPTER 14

Finding Government Web Sites

Along with various educational institutions, the U.S. federal government was instrumental in creating and shaping the Internet and the Web. In the United States, the Internet started with ARPAnet, a government-sponsored network for Defense Department research. It was created in 1969 and grew through the 1970s as more research institutions realized its usefulness. In 1983 this government system adopted the TCP/IP protocol, making it easier to expand the network worldwide. By the early 1990s, as the popularity of the Web started to take off, various U.S. government agencies such as NASA and the National Science Foundation were already on line with some of the most extensive and well-established resources available.

Finding these resources is easy because there is such a wide variety, and also because of the sheer volume. There are so many, in fact, that there are sites for people working in nearly every field and supplying information on just about any topic. Some of these resources, such as NASA and the USGS, have already been mentioned in previous chapters as they relate to educational Web sites.

This chapter will explore some other well-established government resources, such as those at the federal level, as well as some that are relatively new to the Web, such as the various state, local, and city government sites.

How to Find Civic and Municipal Web Resources

Though many federal government agencies have been on the Web for many years, civic and local departments and agencies have only just recently added Internet and Web presence to their plans. This is mostly due to scarce resources and the fact that the Web has only recently emerged as an effective means to reach people on a purely local level. Finding these resources is often a matter of starting with your own local Internet Service Provider (ISP).

▶ **1** Many local governments receive their Internet access the same way the public does, by contracting with local ISPs. Often only the largest metropolitan areas are able to justify the expense of maintaining their own Internet equipment and engineering staff. Start with the home page of the ISP providing your service. Often, your ISP will provide a list of local links as a public service, even if it is not the city's ISP.

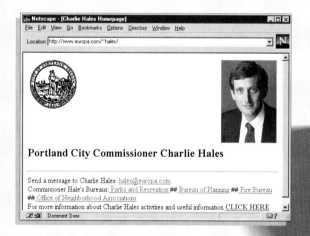

5 If you're lucky, you may even be able to pinpoint the exact civic representative in charge of your favorite city government service through the Web. The Portland, Oregon list of neighborhood associations, for instance, has a link to Commissioner Charlie Hales's Web page, because he is the city representative responsible for the Portland office of neighborhoods. Commissioner Hales's Web page is at http:// www.europa.com/~hales. To find out more about neighborhood association activities, nationally, or for links to your own community, go to the Neighborhoods Online: National Web site at http://www.libertynet.org/community/phila/natl.html.

TIP SHEET

▶ It may be easier to find city information Web sites maintained by private agencies or tourism and visitors associations. These sites often connect to official city government Web resources.

▶ In some cases, city, county, and municipal resources are not Web pages per se, but are Gopher sites or other Internet resources. Most browsers can easily access these resources as well.

2 If you are not connected through a local ISP, you can find a list of links to private ISP home pages in your area through a resource that will also take you directly to lists of local, regional, and state government links. City.Net is a comprehensive international guide to communities around the world and is located at http://www.city.net/. Follow their directory path starting with Country, then State, then City.

3 Another fine resource for locating city government resources in your area is the USA CityLink project at http:// banzai.neosoft.com/citylink/. CityLink's directory pathways are also logically formatted and easy to follow. Just click on your state and you'll see a list of city resources.

Scroll down the page to find local government resources for your state.

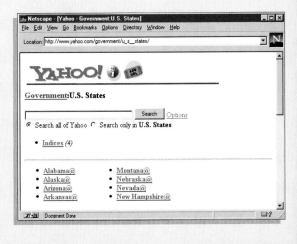

4 Of course, there is always Yahoo, which has a comprehensive list of links in categories and subcategories going from country to region to state to municipality. If you can't find a Web site for your local city government office or agency here, it probably doesn't exist yet. Start at http://www.yahoo.com/Regional/ U.S.States/ and go from there.

How to Find State Government Web Resources

City government sites may still be limited on the Web, but every state in the union now has some sort of Web presence, either as an official state government–run site or commissioned through a private contractor. Finding these state government sites is usually much easier than finding civic sites. And many of the resources listed on the previous page for finding city resources also work well at the state level. Here are some other ways to find state government resources.

1 One way to find government sites on any one of the varous search engines is by searching on the topic *law* (another good one is *politics*). The WWW Virtual Library is one resource with an excellent list of state government servers (state government–run computers with Internet access) under the heading Law: State Government Servers. The URL for the WWW Virtual Library is http://www.law.indiana.edu/law/states.html.

TIP SHEET

▶ **Finding state government resources on the Web can be approached in many different ways. The most straightforward is to look for the name of the state itself with your favorite search engine. Other methods of finding what you need include searching by the keywords "legislation," "state-law," "state-politics," or "state-services."**

▶ **The Web and the Internet offer an easy way to give your favorite (or most hated) state legislator or government offical direct feedback. Nearly every state government page includes either a form to fill out, an e-mail link, or an e-mail address you can use to send messages quickly and directly to the parties who need to hear the voice of the people.**

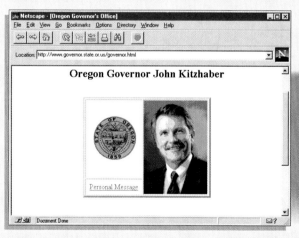

5 Nearly every state government web site either includes information from the Governor's office on the main state home page or has a separate page dedicated to presenting information by and about the Governor. A good example is Oregon Governor John Kitzhaber's home page at http://www.governor.state.or.us/governor.html. This is good way to see who you elected and what they say they are doing to serve you.

2 Another very straightforward, no-frills list of state resources can be found at the State and Local Government on the Net site, at http://www.webcom.com/~piper/state/states.html.

3 Since there are so many different reasons why you might want to contact a state government Web site, the National Association of State Information Resource Executives (NASIRE) has done a bit of the legwork for you. They offer a Web site that allows you to start with the category of state service you're interested in (for example, education, health and welfare, or tourism), and then gives a listing of the Internet resources related to that topic within each state. The URL is http://www.state.ky.us/nasire/NASIREhome.html.

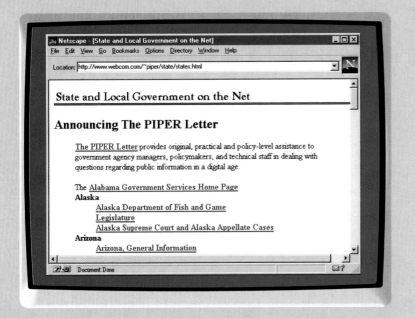

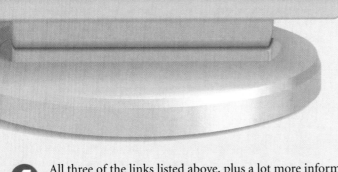

4 All three of the links listed above, plus a lot more information, can be found at the Library of Congress State and Local Governments page at http://lcweb.loc.gov/global/state/state-gov.html. In addition to lists of indexes, this site also has a complete list of links to all the U.S. states' Web sites and a nice state map resource (from the Planet Earth Home Page).

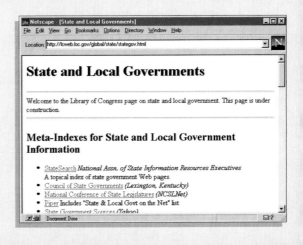

How to Find Federal Government Services on the Web

Because the amount of federal government resources on the Web is so overwhelming, we'll focus strictly on locating services and officials, and then present some of the best examples of each in this and the next section. Let's start with the services.

1 One of the most extensive federal government Web sites (and complete Internet resources) is maintained by the CIA. The World Fact Book is one of the CIA's most popular resources; it provides basic information about every country on the planet, from information on politics and government to tourism, economy, and every other conceivable perspective. The CIA home page is at: http://www.odci.gov/cia/.

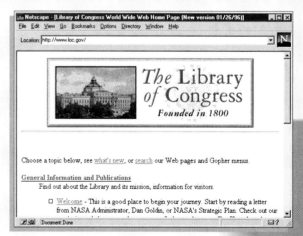

5 The Library of Congress is another meta-index of government resources on the Internet. It is also a museum of American history, an online database for government reports and publications, and a whole lot more. It was founded in 1800 and has kept up with the times in splendid fashion with its well-known Web resource. The URL is http://www.loc.gov/.

TIP SHEET

▶ **Don't forget that Yahoo (http://www.yahoo.com) also has a comprehensive list of links to federal government resources. Just click on the Government listing on the Yahoo home page.**

▶ **The Lycos search engine also has an extensive list of links to government resources at all levels. Lycos's Government directory is organized by topic from Agencies to Resources. The URL is http://www.lycos.com. Just click on the Government link on the Lycos home page.**

2 The Smithsonian Institution is equally famous on the Web for its extensive resources. These include the National Museum of American Art, the National Museum of Natural History, and the National Air & Space Museum, to name only a few. You can spend all week at this one site alone. The URL is http://www.si.edu/.

3 NASA maintains another, even more extensive Web resource. If you can spend a week at the Smithsonian, you can Web-surf a month without ever leaving NASA-related pages. The subcategories are too numerous even to mention—just check it out for yourself. The URL is http://www.nasa.gov/.

4 The next federal resource to make our top 5 list is the the FedWorld Information Network maintained by the National Technical Information Service (NTIS), an agency of the U.S. Department of Commerce. FedWorld is a must-have URL for anyone seeking information about the U.S. federal government. It has both Web and FTP resources and lists of links organized by topic from Aeronautics to Veterans' Affairs. The URL is http://www.fedworld.gov/.

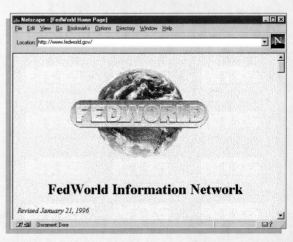

How to Find Federal Government Officials on the Web

Democracy works best when the citizenry is constantly aware of what its elected officials are up to. Today there are federal government Web resources that allow you to communicate with and check up on the officials and lawmakers that you sent to Washington. These federal government sites are just some of the many Web and Internet resources available from the federal government. Since it would be impossible to do justice to this category without a separate book, we'll simply show you some highlights.

1 The most obvious place to start is at the top. The White House home page is very well designed, complete with a guest book and multimedia audio greetings from the President and Vice-President. The URL is http://www.whitehouse.gov/.

TIP SHEET

▶ **Development of a new government information service is underway at the time of this writing. The Government Information Locator Service (GILS) was initiated as the result of the recent U.S. policy to support the information superhighway; the home page (under construction) is located at http://www.usgs.gov/gils/.**

▶ **Another fun way to find your way around the halls of power in Washington, D.C. is a clickable image map at http://www.whitehouse.gov/White_House/EOP/html/DC_map.html. It shows a birds-eye view of the core D.C. area with a listing of the buildings and the offices and branches of government housed inside.**

4 The Legislative Branch is also on the Web in the form of the U.S. House of Representatives Home Page at http://www.house.gov/ (above) and the U.S. Senate home page at http://www.senate.gov/ (below). These resources can direct you to your particular congressional representative as well as help you keep tabs on their activities in congress.

From the White House home page, click on the Executive Branch icon. This will take you to links to all the Cabinet members and their departments, as well as independent federal agencies and commissions set up through the office of the President.

The Legislative Branch of the government is well represented by the Thomas (as in Jefferson) page. It includes the full text of bills from the 103rd and 104th congressional sessions, cross-referenced by branch (Senate or House), sponsor or co-sponsor, and committee. The URL is http://thomas.loc.gov/.

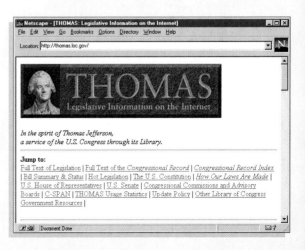

CHAPTER 15

Finding Business Web Sites

In the early days of the Internet it was a generally understood code of conduct not to abuse the privilege of Net access as a means to make money—that is, selling stuff on the Net was frowned on. But as the popularity of the Web started to explode in the early 1990s, the potential for advertising, marketing, customer support, and sales was just too great to keep the free enterprise system at bay for long.

Now the Web is developing into a marketing mainstay for some companies, especially those in computer and telecommunications based industries, and is emerging as a necessary tool to add to the list of advertising options along with point-of-sale, print, and broadcast media for just about every firm with a comprehensive marketing strategy.

But business use, of course, is not limited to sales and marketing alone. The Web and the Internet have always been known for vast and immediate information retrieval and this capability is as valuable for the business community as it is for the halls of science, education, and government.

The amount of business-related news and information available on the Web has now grown to rival even the largest library reference desk. Furthermore, because the information is often updated on a daily basis from tens of thousands of different sources (not just one tired librarian), the Web is usually the most up-to-the-minute source for stock quotes, market reports, financial data, and legal and legislative news from every corner of the globe.

How to Find Web Resources for Business News

Many established print media sources for business news in the "real" world (such as the *Wall Street Journal* or *Business Week* magazine) have found it necessary to add a Web or online component to their services in order to stay competitive. In addition, some new players have entered the scene with purely Web/Internet-based business news resources.

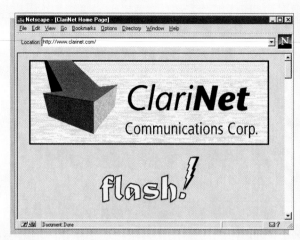

1 One of the most frequented Web resources for daily business news is ClariNet. It is an electronic newspaper with information on a variety of topics, but its business news section is extensive, with current financial information, stock quotes, computer industry news and much more. The URL is http://www.clarinet.com/. Check out the e.News feature with access to ClariNet's substantial list of Usenet newsgroups. (Users of Netscape Navigator 2.0 can use the built-in news reader capability.)

TIP SHEET

▸ **Of course the top Web search engines offer major category listings for business resources, and business news is often one of the largest subcategories under business. This is certainly the case for the Yahoo search engine (http://www.yahoo.com). In the Galaxy search resource, follow the Business General Resources listing under Business and Commerce (http://galaxy.einet.net/).**

▸ **For specific company profile information, the Hoover Reference Library Company Profiles (http://www.quote.com/info/hoover.html) is a comprehensive and up-to-date source with an overview of company operations and strategy and a myriad of details about thousands of corporations worldwide.**

5 A few Web magazines have a purely business-news focus. One is BusinessLink Magazine, developed as a graduate student project at Northwestern University. Its URL is http://www.medill.nwu.edu/businesslink/. Another is the Web version of *Business Week* magazine at http://www.enews.com/magazines/bw/. Both sites feature up-to-date business news and resources.

2 One of the most respected names in business news worldwide is Reuters, and their online presence continues the tradition of complete business news coverage. Their news service, Reuters Business Briefing, offers direct online access to the vast Reuters databases. For a free trial subscription see the Reuters home page at http://www.ib.be/reuters/.

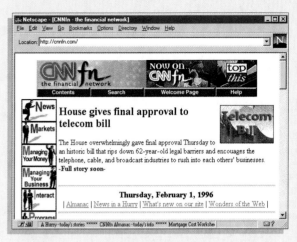

3 The broadcast media aren't interested in being left behind in the rush to get online, and the CNNfn (financial network) is an example of one broadcast-based media source that offers extensive business news coverage on the Web. The CNNfn is at http://cnnfn.com/.

4 As for traditional print media on the Web, the *Wall Street Journal* also does an excellent job of transferring its comprehensive and well-respected business news coverage to cyberspace. The Wall Street Journal home page is at http://www.wsj.com/.

How to Find Financial News on the Web

Every one of the business news sources listed in the previous section has a subsection or component for financial news. No online business news source would be complete without access to current stock reports and financial information. The sites in this section, however, either function exclusively in the area of business markets and investments, or have that as their primary focus.

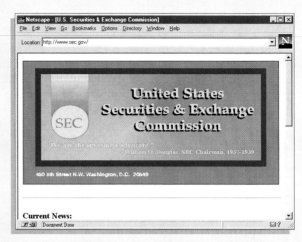

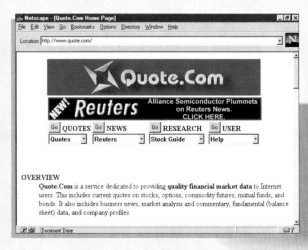

▶ **1** One entity that is certainly focused on investors and investing is the U.S. government Securities and Exchange Commission (SEC), who, by the way, also happens to have a pretty well-developed Web site with lots of investor information. The URL is http://www.sec.gov/.

5 Another good resource for market information is Quote.Com. Its URL is http://www.quote.com/.

TIP SHEET

▶ **All of these indices and more can be found via Yahoo (http://www.yahoo.com/) by following the directory path Business and Economy: Markets and Investments.**

▶ **Online commercial investment services such as PC Quote are too numerous to count. To check if your favorite broker is on the Web, see Yahoo's alphabetical list under the directory path Business and Economy: Companies: Financial Services: Investment Services.**

2 A database called EDGAR (Electronic Data Gathering Analysis and Retrieval) maintained by the SEC is also currently available on the Web (http://www.sec.gov/edgarhp.htm) and is packed with information that can help potential investors find out more about particular companies and corporations.

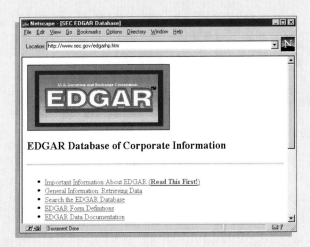

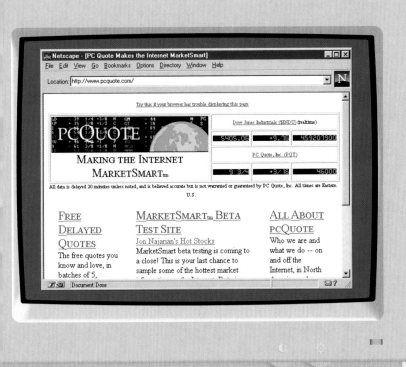

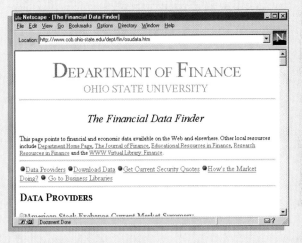

3 Ohio State University maintains an extensive Web site with links to a variety of investment information sources, including the American Stock Exchange and Wall Street Directory, as well as links to a long list of sources for downloadable financial data from S&P, Dow Jones, and many more. The URL is http://www.cob.ohio-state.edu/dept/fin/osudata.htm.

4 A well-presented Internet-exclusive resource for market information is called PC Quote. It shows active market information from the Dow Jones Industrials and is introducing a new service called MarketSmart that will offer up-to-the-minute market information online. The URL is http://www.pcquote.com/.

How to Find Fortune 500 Companies on the Web

One of the fastest growing parts of the Web is the business community, especially among the large corporations who rely on speedy exchange of information to maintain a competitive edge. Many of these larger corporations have a Web site you can visit, and *all* of the corporations in the United States and around the world are profiled by a number of good Web resources. We'll discuss two of them here: the Web 100 listing and the Fortune 500 resource site.

1 The Web 100 source was created just for the purpose of finding big companies. It maintains a listing of the 100 largest U.S. companies on the Web. The URL is http://fox.nstn.ca/~at_info/.

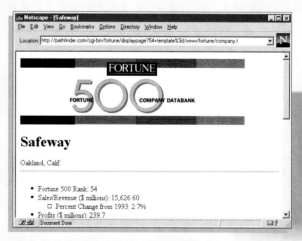

5 The Fortune 500 Company Databank returns a complete data sheet on your company selection, including information about the company's ranking on the list; sales, revenue, and profits figures for the last year reported; and data on the company's stock earnings.

TIP SHEET

▸ **The Fortune 500 site also maintains the complete list of the Fortune 500 companies as well as other information in Adobe Acrobat downloadable file form. This format is true to the graphics and design of the printed magazine and can be found at the following URL http://www. pathfinder.com/fortune/magazine/ specials/fortune500/f500.html.**

▸ **You can also download complete spreadsheets with detailed company information in Mac or PC format from the same URL as above.**

2 Of course, the company for which the Fortune 500 list is named, *Fortune* magazine, has an extensive Web presence (http://www.pathfinder.com/ fortune/fortune.html). The actual Fortune 500 list can be found under the Special Issues section.

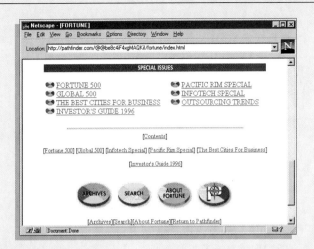

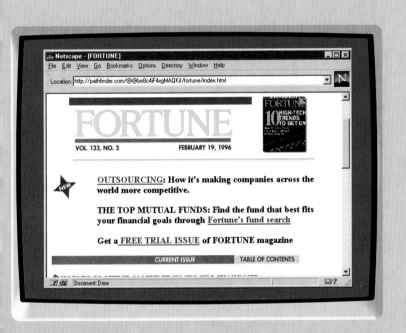

Click here to see the current ranking by revenue.

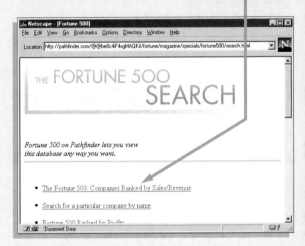

3 The Fortune 500 Web site maintains several different ways to access the company list database. If you want to see what the current ranking is (by revenue), go to the Fortune 500 Search and click on the top link, as shown in the figure.

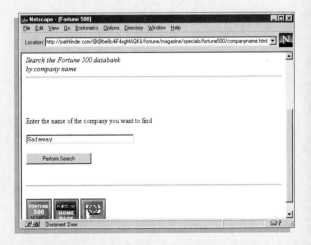

4 You can also search the database to pinpoint the company about which you are inquiring by clicking on the "Search for a particular company by name" link. This takes you to a new page for the Fortune 500 search database. Enter a company name and click on the Perform Search button.

How to Find Cottage Industries on the Web

One nice thing about the Web is that it provides a way to locate unique services and specialty firms in every corner of the globe. By using a few handy business locator sources, you can usually find someone who specializes in whatever product or service you are seeking. You may also discover new and interesting companies offering services or products that you were never previously aware of.

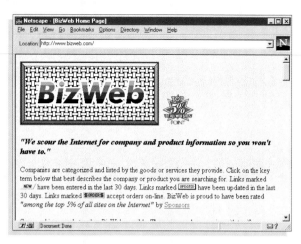

1 One nice source for finding companies both big and small on the Web is called BizWeb and is located at http://www.bizweb.com/. Their database contains over 1,200 companies in dozens of categories from automotive to video.

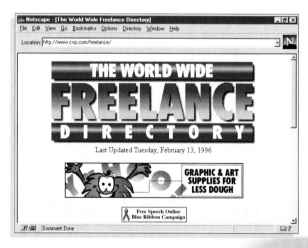

5 The World Wide Freelance Directory is one of the few truly small-business focused lists on the Web. With listings for several skills categories, from advertising to writing and editing to HTML Web page production, this site has over 130 listings so far and is growing. Its URL is http://www.cvp.com/freelance.

TIP SHEET

▶ **The Web is also a rich source of business-to-business resources, with support centers and information resources for starting a business, keeping it growing, and finding suppliers and services. An excellent place to start is Access Business Online at http://www.clickit.com/touch/home.htm.**

▶ **Several niche business resources are also available online to point users to businesses with particular social agendas and interests. Among these are the Christian Business Directory (http://www.xmission.com/~ip/cbd.html) and the African American Business Directory (http://www.scbbs.com/~unite-us/).**

2 Reaching beyond the borders of the United States is the U.K.-based resource called The Biz at http://www.the-biz.co.uk/. More than an extensive list of businesses on the Web listed by category, this resource offers business tips and information, events listings, and much more.

3 Another directory to help you find businesses all over the world, from fashion photographers in South Africa to music lessons in Canada, the Pronet International Directory has just about every business listing you may need wherever you may go. The URL is http://www.pronett.com/.

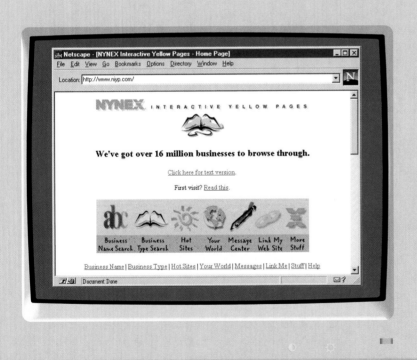

4 For a targeted search of businesses in specific areas, the NYNEX Interactive Yellow Pages is an exhaustive resource boasting over 16.5 million business listings across the United States. With an entry-based search request form, you can find businesses listed by state or by type, or even find a particular business if you know its name but don't know if it's on the Internet. The URL is http://www.niyp.com/.

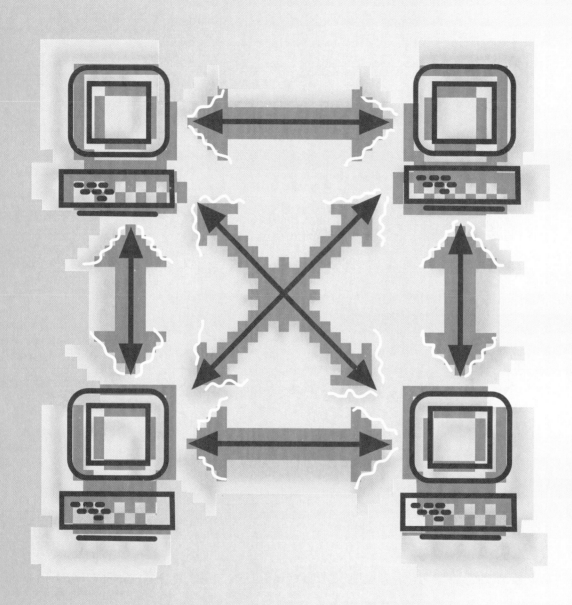

CHAPTER 16

Commerce on the Web

 Some say that the modem is the best thing to happen to shopping since the cash register. And the Web, because of its multimedia environment, is making the biggest splash in the business community of any online resource available.

Shopping on the Web is easy, fast, and fun, and it helps the environment by providing an alternative to the paper catalog. Combine this with the emerging Web technology for video, sound, and 3-D virtual reality, and we may even see some pretty serious competition for shopping malls soon.

On the Web it is as easy to locate those hard-to-find specialty items as it is to find the everyday necessities. Even grocery stores are experimenting with online shopping and are discovering the need for a Web presence.

There are currently thousands of places to shop online, and as with any "real" shopping experience, it is important to have a sense of *caveat emptor*—buyer beware. The virtual storefront makes it even easier to trump up claims of complete and total satisfaction and deliver sub-par goods and services. But for every huckster on the Web, there are hundreds of reputable dealers of products and services of all kinds waiting to provide you with whatever your heart desires—if the price is right.

How to Buy Things on the Web

Many people are concerned about the issue of safety when purchasing something through the Internet with a credit card. There are a number of methods available for purchasing goods and services online other than through credit card transactions, but the technology for securely transferring credit card numbers has reached the point where it is as safe and convenient as using your credit card at the shopping mall. The key for securely transferring credit card numbers or other sensitive information via the Internet is encryption technology. *Encryption* simply means encoding information so that no one other than the intended recipient can decode the message. There are many Web resources that explain encryption in further detail as it relates to specific products or services in the ever-expanding Web marketplace.

TIP SHEET

▶ **For a complete list of Internet resources on this topic, check out Commerce Introductory Material at http://gopher.econ.lsa.umich.edu/EconInternet/Commerce.html. It includes links to many of the services mentioned in this section as well as Michael Peirce's site and dozens of other resources exploring different aspects of Internet commerce and doing business on the Web.**

▶ **With its latest release, Netscape has enhanced the security capabilities of its browser software. For information related to the secure transfer of information see the page located at http://home.mcom.com/comprod/products/navigator/version_2.0/index.html. Other software companies with Web browsers are changing their products to meet the demand for secure online transactions: Call your vendor or check its Web site for the latest news.**

 One group using encryption technology is the Digicash Company, the creators of ecash. *Ecash* is digital money—money that is stored and exchanged as digitized information through computer networks. The concept works in much the same way as withdrawing money from an ATM and then spending it at a local store. First you make a deposit at a bank that processes ecash, just as you would make a deposit at any bank. Then, using custom software, you withdraw a certain amount of ecash and store it on your local computer. You can then spend this digital money at any shop accepting ecash, without having to open an account there first or having to transmit credit card numbers. The Digicash Web site explains the process in detail and also has links to download the software you need as well as find shops that accept ecash. The URL is http://www.digicash.com/.

2 Another group using encryption is CyberCash. Like ecash, CyberCash relies on the use of custom software for encrypting and processing purchase information between a buyer and an online merchant. But unlike ecash, the CyberCash concept relies on the secure transfer of credit card information. A complete explanation of the CyberCash system, a link to CyberCash merchants, and the software to use CyberCash are all available at the following URL: http://www.cybercash.com/.

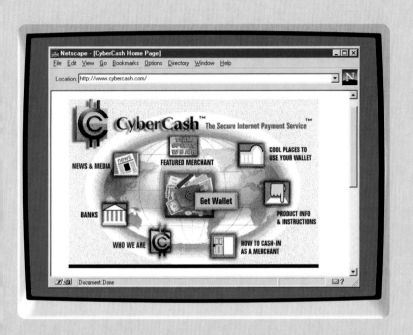

3 Some companies focus on the process of buying and selling strictly digital information, such as images, software, and other products that can be delivered directly to the buyer through the Internet. Often these companies do not use encryption technology because the actual billing is not processed through the Internet. One such company is First Virtual. Before making a purchase, a customer opens a First Virtual account. When a buyer purchases and receives a digital product by downloading it to his or her computer, the seller informs First Virtual and provides information about the transaction, such as the price of the item and the buyer's First Virtual account number. First Virtual then asks the buyer, via e-mail, to confirm that he or she agrees to purchase the product. If the buyer confirms the purchase, then the transaction is recorded on the buyer's First Virtual account. Later, on a regular billing and reporting cycle, First Virtual bills the buyer's designated credit card for all charges accumulated to date. A complete description of the process and links to First Virtual merchants can be found at http://www.fv.com/.

4 A powerful partnership combining the resources of Visa and Microsoft has produced STT (Secure Transactions Technology) which is designed to establish a standard for software used in the secure transfer of electronic information such as credit-card numbers. STT offers banks and merchants the ability to tailor the look and feel and other vital features of the software that their customers use to do business with them. Operating behind the scenes is software code that conforms to the Secure Transaction Technology specifications. This code uses encryption technology that ensures that messages containing bank card numbers and other information are strictly confidential. A complete STT Primer can be found at http://www.visa.com/visa-stt/stt-primer/primer-cov.html.

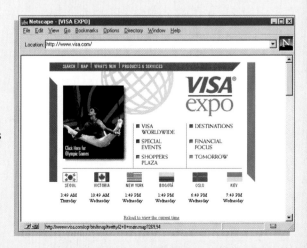

How to Find Shopping Areas on the Web

While the kinks in the money-transfer process get smoothed out, dozens of new Web-based shopping areas are emerging to service the anticipated hordes of online shoppers. They offer a nice alternative to the crowds, parking problems, and elevator music offered at most conventional shopping malls. And even if you can't feel the softness of a fabric or dig through a pile of shirts in the bargain bin, you can still see, hear, and experience a virtual shopping world that continues to grow and evolve on a daily basis.

1 Shopping areas like MarketplaceMCI offer deals on everything from mixing bowls to laptop computers. The alphabetical list of stores affiliated with this on-line center is extensive and includes names you may recognize, like Lillian Vernon and Foot Locker, and some you may have never heard of before. The URL is http://www.internetmci.com/marketplace.

TIP SHEET

▶ **Yahoo (http://www.yahoo.com) maintains a huge list of Internet shopping centers as well as a variety of other business and commerce listings. The listing is alphabetical and includes many categories from advertising to vending machines. The directory path is Business and Economy: Companies.**

▶ **If you want to find out which merchants in your area have an online presence, Yahoo offers a regionally focused business listing. The directory path for this list is Business and Economy: Business Directory: Other Business Directories: Regional.**

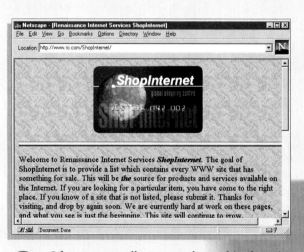

5 Of course, not all stores are located in shopping malls, and the same goes for cyberstores. The ShopInternet site from Renaissance Internet Services is among the resources offering links both to online malls and individual stores listed alphabetically by category. The categories cover everything you might expect, from arts, to computers, to health and beauty aids. The URL for ShopInternet is http://www.ro.com/ShopInternet/.

2 One of the first successful Web shopping areas was the Internet Shopping Network, or ISN. This site tends to lean most heavily toward computer products, with daily deals on everything from hard drives to modems, but it also features links to some well-known specialty stores offering everything from flowers to telephones. The URL is http://www.internet.net/.

3 Some online shopping areas also provide a place for individuals to post "for sale" notices in a newspaper want-ads style. Among these is the JJ Electronic Plaza, which also offers links to a bevy of vendors providing the obligatory computer products as well as a few specialty items, such as rare and vintage record albums and underwater diving-mask lenses. The URL is http://www.jjplaza.com/.

4 The iMall, from Electronic Marketing Services, is an example of a Web-commerce environment that features stores set up to accept your purchases online. Many still rely on phone ordering though 800 numbers, but a few shops at the iMall use some of the payment schemes presented on the previous page for immediate and secure Internet purchasing. The URL is http://www.imall.com/.

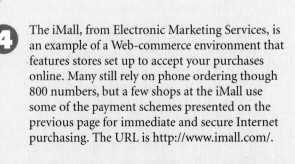

How to Find Customer Support Web Sites

Many companies are realizing that the Web is an excellent place to provide customer service and support; successful companies rely on repeat sales that only come with ongoing customer satisfaction. And the Web can offer a 24-hour post-purchase support presence that is available seven days a week and is even open on holidays. Companies use the Web to provide free components that can enhance a certain product, product background and late-breaking information on new features, and a ready feedback capability for fielding requests for information, complaints, and general comments from customers.

TIP SHEET

► Whenever you buy new software or computer hardware products, you are almost guaranteed to find an online resource created by the manufacturer. Even the smallest of companies in this industry understands the importance of having some online presence, if not a fully developed Web site. Check the printed materials in your packaging or instructions for a URL or other Internet address, even if it is only an e-mail address. This is a great way to get the lastest updates, free add-on products, or immediate technical assistance.

► More and more travel agencies, airlines, hotels, and motels are beginning to develop helpful Web sites and Internet resources. If you are planning a trip somewhere, take a look at the travel and accomodation Web sites related to your destination. It may save you some time in transit or help you get the most out of your journey. If you have booked your flight already, you may be able to check the airline's Web site to see what resources are available at your destination.

1 Because of the nature of the medium, computer and electronics companies were among the first to develop customer support Web sites. Many of these offer free software updates for use with computer products, technical advice or online access to technical support people, and links to related products and services. Some of the most extensive and highly developed of these sites are Apple Computers at http://www.apple.com/; IBM at http://www.ibm.com/; Intel at http://www.intel.com/; Motorola at http://www.motorola.com/; Tektronix at http://www.tektronix.com/; Hewlett-Packard at http://www.hp.com/; Toshiba at http://www.toshiba.com/; Texas Instruments at http://www.ti.com/; and Compaq Computers at http://www.compaq.com/.

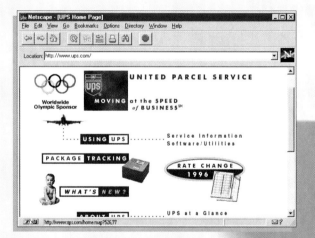

4 Of course, the service industries are every bit as active on the Web as the retailers and product manufacturers. Some have won awards for their Web sites in terms of overall look and "feel," but many have also begun to use the Web as new way to reach out to new customers or provide a new way for current customers to order services or get assistance. Among the leaders in this area are United Parcel Service at http://www.ups.com/; Federal Express (FedEx) at http://www.fedex.com/; Southwest Airlines at http://www.iflyswa.com/; Coldwell Banker Real Estate at http://www.coldwellbanker.com/; and ITT Sheraton Hotels at http://www.sheraton.com/

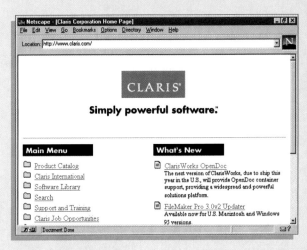

2 All of the largest computer software companies also have Web sites, many of which are as extensive and sophisticated as their computer hardware counterparts. These sites also offer the requisite customer support options, free tidbits and software updates that add value to the customer's initial software purchase. These sites include Microsoft at http://www.microsoft.com/; Adobe Systems at http://www.adobe.com/; Macromedia at http://www.macromedia.com/; Claris Corporation at http://www.claris.com/; and Novell at http://www.novell.com/.

3 Some of the most well-known merchants are also getting into the act with Web sites that feature products, catalogs, store listings (for nationwide and worldwide outlets), and general company information, making it easy to contact the retailer for returns, questions, and comments. Among the most extensive and interesting sites are F.A.O. Schwarz at http://www.faoschwarz.com//; J.C. Penney at http://www.jcpenny.com/; FTD Florists at http://www.ftd.com/; and Wal-Mart at http://www.wal-mart.com/.

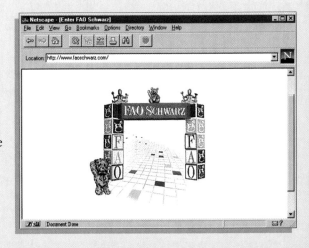

CHAPTER 17

Personal and Social Web Sites

 The Web has been deluged with people interested in exploring this new medium for strictly social purposes. And with such limitless options and ease of access it is no wonder that this genre of activity has exploded in popularity.

The Internet has always been a safe and handy way for people to connect over long distances, but for some it has created a whole new way to hang out and develop a completely new social circle. The increased use of Internet Relay Chat channels has taken some service providers by storm, and many of them are struggling to provide enough bandwidth to support the demand. And the Web has become a handy medium for clans of IRC enthusiasts to post bulletin board–type notices and updates for people who like to frequent particular IRC channels.

The Web has also emerged as a convenient way for people to meet other people through personal ads and dating or matchmaking services. The Web allows for as much or as little disclosure of personal data as the user chooses to share. It also creates the kind of computer database environment that allows people to specify the particular attributes they are looking for in a partner through searchable entry forms.

A few of the most popular ways to use the Web for purely social interests are explored in this chapter.

How to Find Individual Home Pages

Individual home pages are some of the most interesting destinations on the Web. They are the expressions of individuality that have come to define and embody the flavor of the Internet as a whole. Finding these pages is often a random occurrence, but they can yield some of the richest treasures. You may even make some new friends who share your interest in, say, pet iguanas. There is no best way to find these pages, nor is there any particular step-by-step process, but these four suggestions will get you started.

▶ ❶ Yahoo's directory shows a list of individual home pages, each one added by request of the people who created them. There is no arbiter of taste or style here (as you will soon find out), but this freedom fuels a wide range of expression. This list is huge—be prepared for some download time. It even includes Santa Claus's home page during the holidays (over half a dozen of them, actually—can you find the real one?). The URL for Yahoo is http://www.yahoo.com/, and the path is Society and Culture: People: Personal Home Pages. One interesting home page found here, which belongs to Robert Hildebrand, is doc hbrand's wacky site (http://www.sisna.com/hbrand/).

TIP SHEET

▶ **If your ISP is local, it is likely that they will have a list of individual home pages created by people in your area. Take a look around their directory pages and search for a listing of individual clients. You may find that someone you know has a Web page.**

▶ **Though there is no single directory of people on the Web, Yahoo's individual listing is a good place to start if you are looking for someone in particular. Be prepared to be patient, however. Finding an individual on the Web is frightfully similar to searching for the proverbial needle in the haystack.**

2 Many families are finding that the Web is a fun and interesting way to tell the world about little Jimmy's new braces or cousin Arthur's latest exploits in the Philippines. One interesting service is setting up whole cyber neighborhoods full of family pages. The GeoCities project by Beverly Hills Internet has family and individual home pages grouped in several different theme categories, like "Sunset Strip" and "Times Square." It's fun to visit, and you won't have to worry about locking your car. The URL is http://www.geopages.com/.

3 Every ISP likes to show off their list of clients. Many of these lists are now so huge, however, that you are often simply offered a clickable alphabet from which to select at random (or search for people you know by name). Many also offer thumbnail image options for the listee to present a small photo or a cute graphic next to the link to his or her page. This example is from the Europa Service Provider in Portland, Oregon (http://www.europa.com/ users/home-pages.html). (For an extensive list of ISPs, point your browser to ISP Meta-List at http://www. herbison.com/herbison/iap_meta_list.html.)

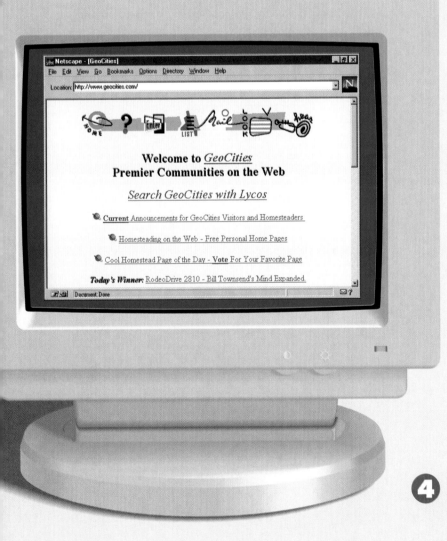

4 One of the most popular sites for finding random home pages is the Birthday Web. If astrologers are to be believed, people who share your birth date may also share some of your basic personality traits. This is a way to find out if that translates into home page creation styles as well. Just plug in your birth date and see who else out there with the same birthday has created a home page. The URL is http://www.boutell.com/birthday.cgi/.

Society and Culture on the Web

E very possible special interest group now seems to have at least one Web site. Web sites are often listed as references for new people interested in joining a particular Usenet newsgroup. They show up in newsgroup postings and they are often referenced in the topic headings of IRC channels. And many Web sites created to support a particular club's activities will list important newsgroup references and IRC channels in return. Now, with the emergence of Netscape Navigator 2.0, IRC, newsgroup, and Web surfing capabilities are all built into one browser, making the process of switching between resources even easier.

1 Some groups with large nationwide or worldwide membership bases have elaborate Web sites covering all aspects of the groups' interests and practices. Among these are religion-based groups with extensive Web resources addressing scripture and doctrine, current issues, history and culture, and much more. The B'nai B'rith Interactive Web site (http://bnaibrith.org/), for example, is a huge compilation of links and Web resources providing information on Jewish culture. James Tucker's Religious Resources Page (http://convex.cc.uky.edu/ ~jatuck00/Religion/Religion.html) has links to and resources for many other religion-based Web sites, from Catholic to Zen-Buddhist, to Hindu, and many general theology references.

TIP SHEET

▶ **Netscape Navigator 2.0 has a built-in news-reader capability, making it as easy to open newsgroups as it is to move between Web pages. If you are not using Navigator, your browser will probably still be able to automatically open a newsreader application if you click on a Usenet link on a Web page, as long as you configure your preferences settings for your helper applications accordingly. Check your browser's documentation for information on configuring newsreader helper applications.**

▶ **Yahoo has a Regional reference that may include a special Clubs and Societies section for your area. Even though many clubs are local and meet in person, they may still have Web pages to share information in a bulletin board style, or to reach out to other clubs and societies with the same interests located in different parts of the world.**

2 The SeniorCom site (http://www.senior.com/) is an example of the expanding reach of the Web and the growing diversity of users plugging into the Internet. Once thought to be the sole domain of scientists and cybersavvy college kids, the Web is now finding a receptive audience among seniors who use sites like SeniorCom to exchange information. SeniorCom offers special chat rooms to meet others and make new friends, as well as access to current information on travel, financial resources, health, fitness, housing, and other areas of special interest to the senior community.

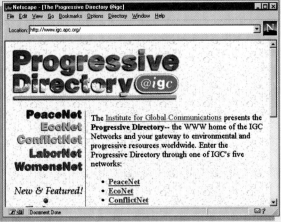

3 Groups from every point on the political spectrum are represented on the Web, as are social interest groups that use the Web for the promotion of issues that cross political, social, and national boundaries. One established Web resource of this type is the Institute of Global Communications, or IGC (http://www.igc.apc.org/), which offers an array of links to affiliated networks focused on peace, environmental protection, human rights, social and economic justice, and a host of other issues. Another good resource for finding nonprofit organizations is the Nonprofit Resources Catalogue at http://www.clark.net/pub/pwalker/.

How to Find Web Sites for Social Gatherings and Chat Groups

If you want to make some new friends but don't necessarily want to join a specific club or special interest group, you can still use the Web as a convenient and interesting place to just hang out. Just as the Web smoothly integrates with Usenet newsgroups for clubs and targeted interests, the Web also smoothly integrates with IRC (Internet Relay Chat) areas for general discussion purposes. Though many IRC channels are devoted to specific topics, a number of them are undefined. Information on how to find and use IRC channels is in abundant supply on the Web.

TIP SHEET

► Netscape Navigator (2.0 and later) has an autoscrolling feaure allowing for the continuous feed of new information such as with a live conversation. This allows Web site creators to build chat functionality directly into an HTML window without having the browser call out to a specific IRC helper application. For more information on this and other expanded features of the Navigator browser for use in live chat environments, see the Netscape home page at http://home.netscape.com/.

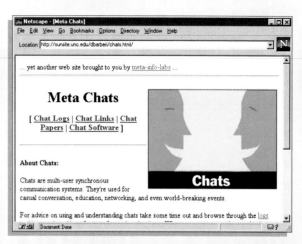

 1 An extensive Web resource on IRC chatting and other direct chat networks is the Synchronous Communications on the Net page at http://sunsite.unc.edu/dbarberi/chats.html. This site has lists of links for finding chat channels, chat software, and logs of discussions on topical issues such as the Oklahoma City bombing or the Presidential election.

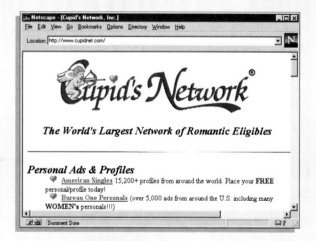

4 The Web is a new and creative way for single people to meet other singles, place personal ads, and find the love of their life. Several interesting Web sites have been developed to cater to this emerging interest. Cupid's Network, for instance, offers free personal profiles and has nearly 9,000 entries at last count. It also has fee-based services that are more elaborate, as well as areas that focus on particular groups such as Christian singles or single parents. The URL is http://www.cupidnet.com/.

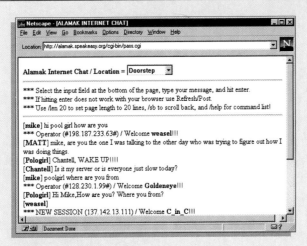

2 Some chat channels are set up specifically for viewing and interacting with a Web browser. As long as your service provider has the right connection (and most do), it is possible to log in to a Web page with a live conversation in progress. You just plug in a nickname for yourself and hit Enter; the screen is refreshed showing your entry into the chat area.

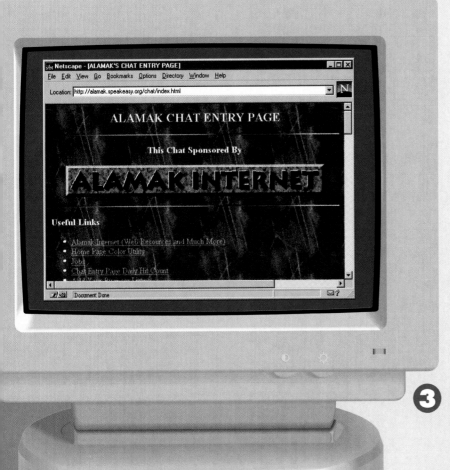

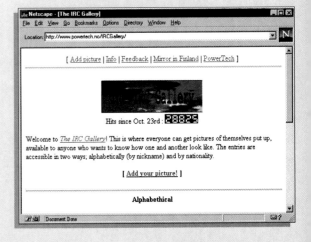

3 Because the IRC environment is basically a scrolling screen where people type messages to each other, the people in the conversation rarely have any idea what the people they are talking to look like. The IRC Gallery Web site was set up to offer visual information about the people you meet online. IRC enthusiasts can post a picture of themselves at this Web site and then refer their fellow conversationalists there to see who they are talking to. The URL is http://www.powertech.no/IRCGallery/.

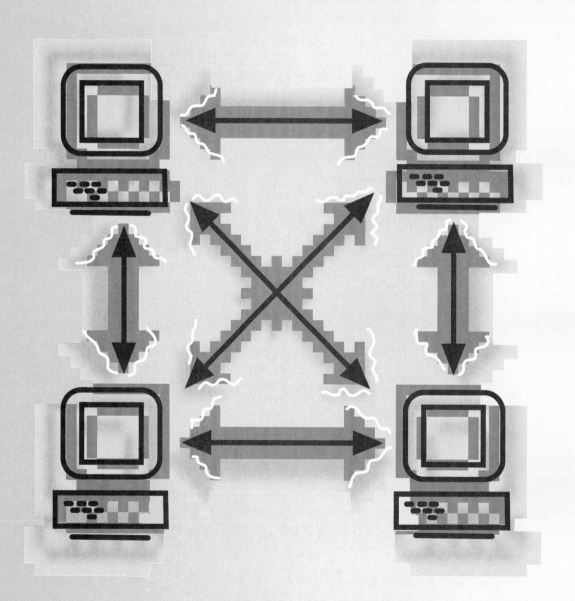

CHAPTER 18

Finding Web Sites for Arts and Literature

Many proponents of arts and literature were quick to see the Web's potential for expanding the cultural awareness of the online populace. One of the first Web sites to become internationally recognized for its contribution to the growth of Web culture was Nicolas Pioch's Web Museum, which started out by placing some of the better known works from the Louvre on the Web. Now the Web Museum has dozens of mirror sites throughout the world and features many more artworks than are housed in any single museum.

Hundreds of commercial and nonprofit arts organizations have followed by bringing thousands of works of art to the Web environment. You can find nearly every style of display art and every kind of art organization on the Web, from the large, well-established museums featuring traditional masterpieces to newer grass-roots arts organizations featuring avant garde and off-the-wall pieces.

As for literature, the Web has quickly become an immense card catalog with hundreds of searchable indexes and guides, making it easy to find just about every book, periodical, and reference work that has ever been published. Nearly every major publishing house has a Web presence, and they all recognize that though the Internet may not be able to completely replace the printed word, it will soon become indispensable for the promotion and distribution of information on published works.

How to Find Art Museums on the Web

Most people get sore feet before they've seen the entire collection of a medium-sized museum, and visiting all the major museums in a city like New York or Paris can be absolutely exhausting. However, the arts community has been quick to embrace Web technology, and it's now possible to see an enormous collection of art, all from the comfort of your swivel chair. Nearly every type of art museum and style of art is currently on the Web. Here are a few of the first and largest museums currently on the Web.

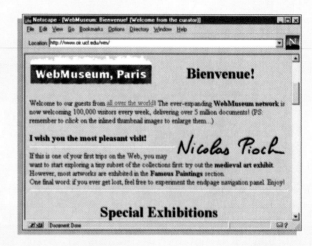

1 The WebMuseum (formerly WebLouvre) is the granddaddy of online museums. Originally this Web site displayed works exclusively from the Louvre Museum in Paris as well as scenes and other information from around Paris. Now the WebMuseum has grown into a cybermuseum that doesn't necessarily focus on works housed at any particular museum. This frees it up to display a variety of works by a variety of artists—from the masters to the latest works of contemporary artists. There are several locations for the WebMuseum; the original location in France is http://mistral.enst.fr/.

5 No presentation of renowned art museums is complete without mentioning the Metropolitan Museum of Art in New York City. And true to form, their Web site is also a doozy. You shouldn't go to New York without visiting the Met, and you shouldn't peruse art museums online without checking out the Met Web site at http://www.metmuseum.org/.

TIP SHEET

► A handy reference to art museums in New York (where many of the best museums are located) and around the world is the NetVillage New York Museums Etc. page at http://www. webcom.com/village/. This reference is not limited to online museums, but it does include current hyperlinks to those with a Web presence.

► Yet another handy reference for finding museums online is the FineArt Forum Online Art Resources Directory at http://www.msstate.edu/Fineart_ Online/art-resources/museums.html.

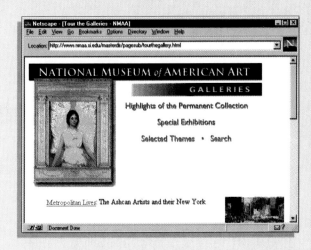

2 The Museum of Modern Art (MOMA) in New York and the SFMOMA in San Francisco both have online exhibits, the SFMOMA site being the more developed of the two. The SFMOMA site can be found at http://www.sfmoma.sf.ca.us/. The New York MOMA site is at http://www.sva.edu/moma/.

3 Walking around Washington, D.C. (especially in summer) can be exhausting, but it is worth it to see some of the greatest art treasures in the world on display at the National Museum of American Art (NMAA). But the Web now offers an alternative to all that walking—the NMAA Web site at http://www.nmaa.si.edu/.

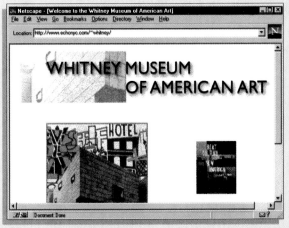

4 Another must-see art museum on the Web is the Whitney Museum of American Art. The actual museum is a masterpiece of architectural design—I recommend visiting the real thing in New York—but if you would like a taste of the collection inside, visit their Web site at http://www.echonyc.com/~whitney/.

How to Find Fine Arts Resources on the Web

The Web has created a whole host of new ways to find and view great works of art by both new and emerging artists and the masters. The online museums mentioned on the previous page provide easy access to a variety of works, but there are many other Web resources that focus on the presentation of works of art from around the world. Many works that will never be displayed in a museum have been given new life and have reached new audiences through the Internet.

 1 One popular resource is the fineArt Forum produced at Griffith University in Queensland, Australia. It is an electronic news service available as a monthly e-mail digest, an online Gopher database, and a colorful Web site. It is managed by a unique virtual organization whose board members meet on the Internet. It has links to many art museums, and it can also direct you to a number of galleries, fine arts festivals and conferences, arts schools, and much more. The URL is http://www.msstate.edu/Fineart_Online/.

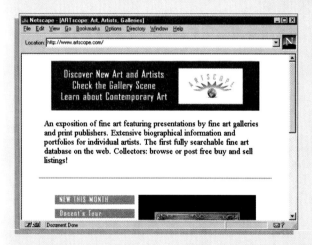

5 Two commercial Web resources, ArtSpeaks and ARTscope, focus primarily on the presentation of artworks and prints for sale and also offer helpful links for finding galleries, dealers, and individual artists online. ArtSpeaks can be found at http://www.artspeaks.com/~artspeak, and ARTscope is at http://www.artscope.com/.

TIP SHEET

▸ In addition to fine art resources, many resources exist on the Web for art history, art in cinema, architecture, performing arts, arts organizations, and much more. The Yahoo search engine (http://www.yahoo.com) has links to many of these resources under the main heading Arts.

▸ Visual presentation is one of the things the Web does best, and as a result a vast number of Web pages are devoted to resources somehow related to the visual arts. Simply plugging in the word *art* as a keyword to search on within any of the search engines (Lycos, WebCrawler, and so on) will often produce a list of links that is too large to be very useful. When looking for art resources, try further defining your keywords by genre, style, time period, or any other limiting factor that can help pinpoint the exact art resource you want.

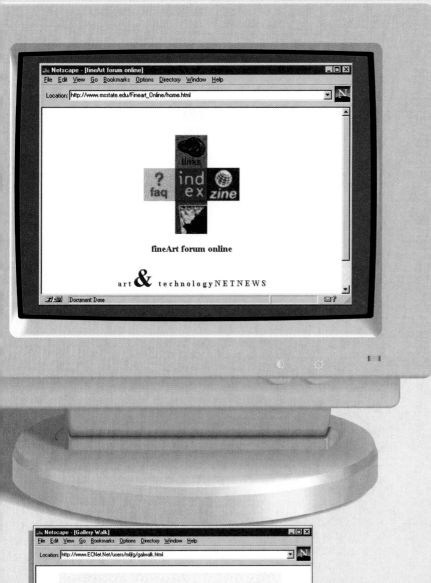

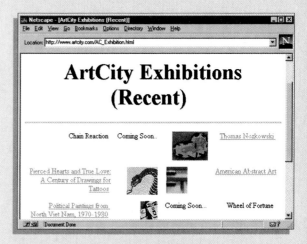

2 Another useful arts resource online is ArtCity, a commercial arts resource organization based in New York. ArtCity has its own exhibition hall (shown here), as well as links to artist resources, galleries and dealers, news and media resources for artists and art enthusiasts, and an "Art For Sale" section for purchasing works of art displayed online. The URL is http://www.artcity.com/.

3 Two more fine arts resources on the Web, artline and artview, both offer extensive lists for finding galleries, dealers, online art sales outlets, and a whole host of other fine arts listings. Artview is the larger of the two resources, with listings of resources both online and in the real world, whereas artline focuses exclusively on online arts resources. The URL for artview is http://www. artview.com/, and the URL for artline is http://www.catalog.com/artline/.

4 Since many art galleries do not yet have Web sites of their own, a few resources such as GalleryWalk have developed Web sites that pull together selected works from various galleries around the world into a single Web location. GalleryWalk is a nonprofit organization with a Web site hosted by the Educational Computing Network (ECN) in Chicago, and it features works from commercial, academic, nonprofit, and independent art galleries. The URL is http://www.ECNet.Net/users/mfjfg/galwalk.html.

How to Find Books on the Web

Some say that the Internet (especially the Web) will rival the Gutenberg press in its impact on society relative to the dissemination of information. Many say that this is the "information age" and the Web is certainly a big part of that claim. Not many people, however, are predicting that the Web will end up replacing the printed word altogether—after all, it is still difficult to cuddle up with a computer to read a novel. But the Web does offer a unique new way to find that novel. This section explores some of the Web resources available for locating books and bookstores around the world.

1 The number of booksellers online is large and growing daily. Since nearly every major bookstore has a computerized ordering system anyway, it makes sense to adapt these book ordering mechanisms to the Internet and the Web. One source of links to booksellers around the world is BookWeb, produced by the American Booksellers Association. This site is loaded with resources for finding books, book news, bookseller services, and much more. The URL is http://www.ambook.org/.

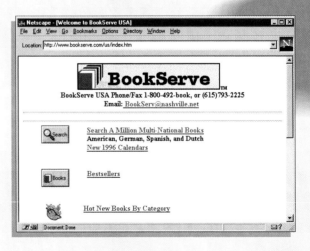

5 One more resource for finding books and publishers online is BookServe. This extensive site has listings of the current bestsellers, an index searchable by author, type of book, and title, and a complete online ordering mechanism as well. The URL is http://www.bookserve.com/.

TIP SHEET

▶ To find electronic texts (books you can read online) and many other book-related sites on the Web, be sure to visit BookWire at http://www.bookwire.com/.

▶ To locate book reviews and online discussions on hot book topics, popular authors, and bestsellers, the Hungry Mind Review at http://www.bookwire.com/hmr/ can't be beat. This site also features nice-looking graphics, as does its online host, BookWire.

2 Of course, with the Web you don't need to have a physical storefront to sell books. Many of the major book publishers are taking their wares directly to the people. The publisher of the book you are looking at right now, for instance (ZD Press/Macmillan Computer Publishing USA), has an extensive Web site featuring many popular titles, complete with online ordering information. The URL is http://www.mcp.com/mcp/.

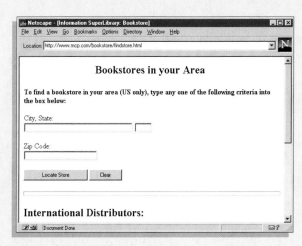

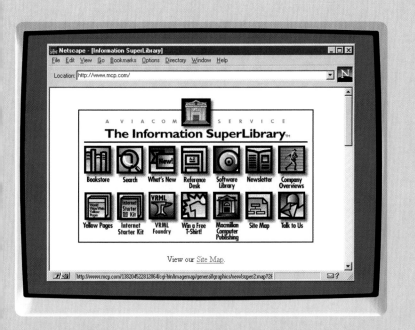

3 The Macmillan site also offers a handy tool for finding bookstores in your area, since many people still like walking into a bookstore and physically picking up books, flipping through them, and smelling fresh ink on the printed page. Enter the following URL: http://www.mcp. com/bookstore/findstore.html. The dialog box pictured above will appear.

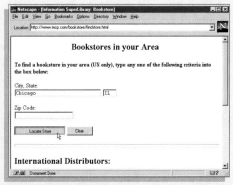

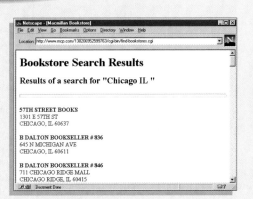

4 Enter your city, state, and zip code in the entry boxes as shown. If you have several zip codes in your city, leave that entry box blank. Click on the Locate Store button. A menu of bookstores for the location you entered will appear, complete with mailing addresses.

How to Find Libraries on the Web

The Web offers extensive listings and links for finding libraries throughout the world. Some of the most sophisticated library Web sites offer online access to their reading material, so when it is rainy, cold, and miserable outside you don't have to brave the weather to find that favorite book or library reference you are seeking.

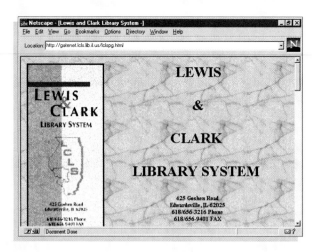

 1 The Lewis & Clark Library in Edwardsville, IL, is an excellent example of a local library's presence on the Web. Its URL is http://gatenet.lcls.lib.il.us/lclspg.html. To find out if your local library is on the Web, check the list maintained by the St. Joseph County Public Library at http://sjcpl.lib.in.us/.

TIP SHEET

▶ An extensive resource listing many online and digital library resources is the Building Digital Libraries page at http://www.texshare.edu/TexShare Services/Professional/digital.html. This site offers a long list of links to information about digital library hardware, software, vendors, and current digital library projects.

▶ For a wealth of information about online books (also called etext) check out the Web site Online Books FAQ. It has information in frequently asked question (FAQ) form, as well as lists of etext books known to be in the public domain (freely available to the public) from such well-known authors as Charles Dickens and Mark Twain. The URL is http://www.cs.indiana.edu/metastuff/bookfaq.html.

5 And, of course, the Library of Congress has an extensive library resource on the Web. One interesting offshoot is the American Memory: Historical Collections for the National Digital Library. This resource provides collections of primary source and archival material relating to American culture and history. The URL is http://lcweb2.loc.gov/amhome.html.

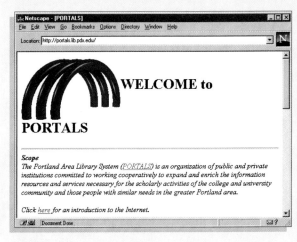

2 PORTALS (Portland Area Library System) is a cooperative effort to put library services online in the Portland, Oregon metropolitan area. This project combines the resources of both a public and a private online library system. Ask your local library if they have a Web site, or better yet, if they share online resources with other library systems. The URL for PORTALS is http://portals.lib.pdx.edu/.

3 The Internet Public Library (IPL) offers many of the same services as local "real" public libraries in a Web environment. IPL has virtual classrooms, exhibits, a reading room, a "card" catalog, youth-directed services and much more. The URL is http://ipl.sils.umich.edu/.

4 As the private sector has become more involved with the Web, a few philanthropic-minded organizations have found it beneficial to provide library-like resources on the Web for the public to use for free. One of the most extensively developed examples of this concept is the IBM Digital Library, which offers digital manuscripts, search and query database resources, and more. The URL is http://www.ibm.com/Features/library/.

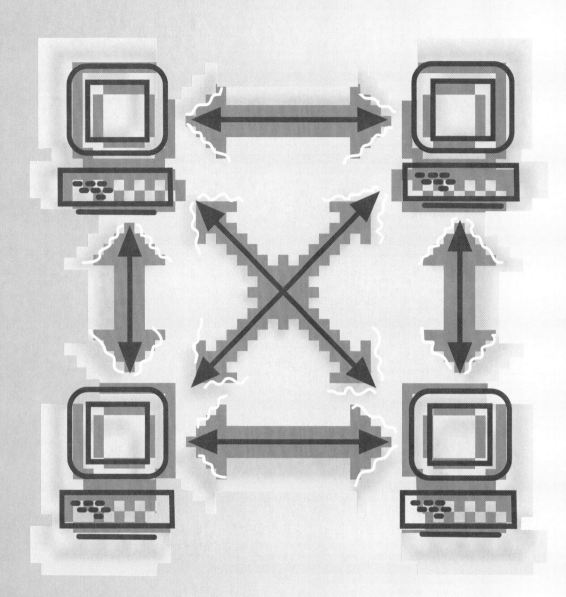

CHAPTER 19

Finding Entertainment Web Sites

 The entertainment industry has found the Web to be an effective new promotional tool. Web sites are often used as a promotional tool along with mainstream advertising, for the larger-budget motion picture releases in the United States. They are a unique way to give people who haven't yet seen a particular film a taste of what they may be missing.

Web sites also give producers of TV shows and movies a way to generate a fan base and support a loyal following, giving people more incentive to tune in week after week or to see a particular movie more than once. In some cases, a loyal following of people will emerge spontaneously and build one or more Web sites as a purely volunteer effort expressing their devotion to a particular show or the principal cast members.

In the music industry, fans of particular bands and artists often create Web sites featuring sound clips, rare photographs, or interesting images of their favorite performers. Some Web sites are part of a coordinated promotional effort generated by the artists themselves and their producers. These will feature touring dates, late-breaking information or upcoming recording release dates, extensive background information about the performers, and ordering information for purchasing CDs, videos, posters, T-shirts, and more.

How to Find Film-Related Web Sites

F inding Web sites for upcoming movies is sometimes as easy as looking carefully at the posters or watching the bottom of your TV screen during the advertisements. Many times a URL will appear showing the Web address of a particular promotional site—often complete with the title of the movie as a custom domain name (http://www.batmanforever.com, for example). For the same reasons that other commercial interests like the Web, movie promoters find this medium to be increasingly popular as well: Web pages are easy to access, available 24 hours a day, and are relatively inexpensive to create and maintain compared to the advertising costs of television spots or space in major newspapers and national magazines.

▶ ❶ Many indices of film and video information exist on the Web. One popular site offering a "critical perspective to the world of film" is film.com. This site contains information on current movie releases, video releases, film festivals, and more, all placed tastefully on a backdrop of a red velvet theater curtain. The URL is http://www.film.com/.

TIP SHEET

▶ **Of course the major motion picture studios aren't the only ones making movies. The Web also offers a new avenue for independent filmmakers to show and promote their work. It is also a great resource for budding film makers to find information, helpful hints, and tips for honing their craft. One such site is the Movie Makers Guild, which is a Macintosh Users Group for kids 12 to 18 who want to learn the first step in making a film, TV commercial, or TV show. The URL is http:// www.el-dorado.ca.us/~dmnews/mmguild.html/.**

▶ **Another fun movie resource is the Movie Quote Homepage, designed for people who can remember a line from a movie but just can't remember what movie it came from. The author of this page is a self-proclaimed movie quote god who is on the Web and ready to help. You can also play a movie quote game from this page—movie buffs will love this stuff. The URL is http:// www.cse.psu.edu/~noonan/movie.html.**

❺ In some cases a movie may be well past its initial release date, but upcoming video release or pay-per-view cable programming justifies continued Web-based promotion. The Batman Forever Web site is one example. The URL is http://www.batmanforever.com.

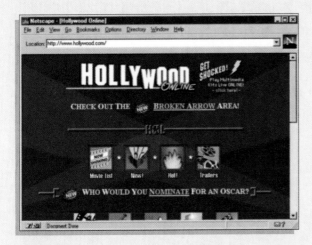

2 Hollywood means movies, whether in the real world or on the Web. Hollywood Online has an extensive Web site featuring interactive multimedia promotional kits, sound bites, photos, and host of other information about current and upcoming movies. The URL is http://www.hollywood.com/.

IMDB mirror sites and other URLs

3 Calling itself "the most comprehensive free source of movie information on the Internet," the Internet Movie Database has been providing movie and entertainment information on the Internet for over five years. This site has grown to include mirror sites in six different countries and features extensive lists of links to film resources worldwide, with information on current releases, video releases, and even films on TV. The URL is http://www.cm.cf.ac.uk/Movies/.

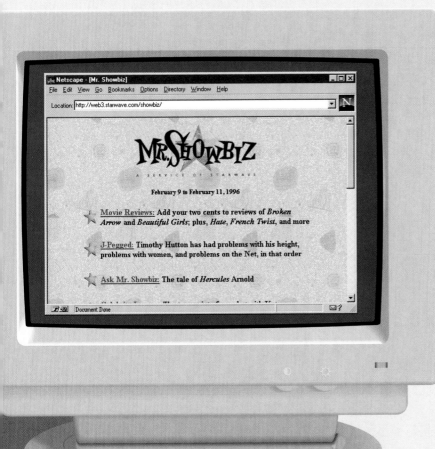

4 One nutty, wacky Web site focusing on current movie and entertainment news and information is Mr. Showbiz. This site features such offbeat items as digital celebrity plastic surgery (morphing celebrity faces), and also offers commentary and criticism, box-office stats for current movie releases, and a place for visitors to share their own applause or catcalls. The URL is http://web3.starwave.com/showbiz/.

How to Find TV Web Resources

A s with movies, more and more television shows are starting to develop corresponding Web sites. This is especially true of educational or information-based shows such as those on public television. Certain cable channels such as the Discovery Channel, CNN, and the Sci-Fi Channel are also pioneering efforts in this area. And one popular Web resource, cInet, has gone the other direction by developing a television program focusing on Web and Internet happenings and information.

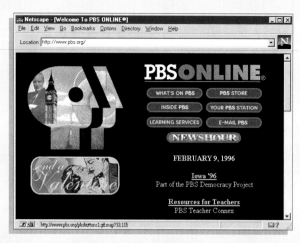

▶ **①** Of course, the major commercial television networks now have fully developed Web sites. These are excellent resources for finding the latest information on your favorite show—or to see if it has been canceled. The URLs for the major U.S. television networks are http://www.abctelevision.com/, http://www.nbc.com/, http://www.cbs.com/, http://www.foxnetwork.com/, and http://www.pbs.org/.

TIP SHEET

▶ **For those deviants who actually enjoy television commercials, there are a few sites devoted solely to presenting more information about TV ads then any normal human being would ever want or need to know. One of the best is the Gallery of Advertising Parody, where "ads that exploit sex, age, baldness, and dirt and grime all find a home." The URL is http://www.dnai.com/~sharrow/parody.html.**

▶ **Many radio stations are also finding that the Web is a nice way to reach out to the listening audience. To date there are over 200 commercial radio stations with Web sites listed with the Yahoo (http://www.yahoo.com) search engine. To see if your favorite radio station has a Web page follow the Yahoo directory path Business and Economy: Companies: Media: Radio: Stations.**

⑤ The Academy of Television Arts & Sciences, which produces the annual Emmy Awards, now has its own official Web site. This site features a wealth of archived information about various TV programs. Its URL is http://www.emmys.org/. The URL for the Museum of Television and Radio is http://www.mtr.org/.

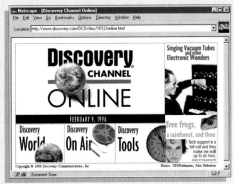

2 The Sci-Fi Channel and the Discovery Channel are two cable channels with Web sites that are fully developed resources for finding more information about programming, schedules, and other program-related topics. The URLs for these and a couple of the other top U.S. cable networks are http://www.scifi.com/ (Sci-Fi Channel), http://www.discovery.com/ (Discovery Channel), http://www.hbohomevideo.com/ (HBO), and http://www.mtv.com/ (MTV).

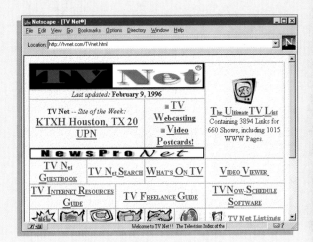

3 There are a number of good Web sites out there that scan all the networks and stations and distill the results into a one-stop Web resource for all your TV info needs. One such site is TV Net, with national and worldwide TV information as well as a handy way to search for programming information in your particular region. The URL is http://tvnet.com/. The Tardis TV Archive is another such handy resource. The URL is http://src.doc.ic.ac.uk/public/media/tv/collections/tardis/.

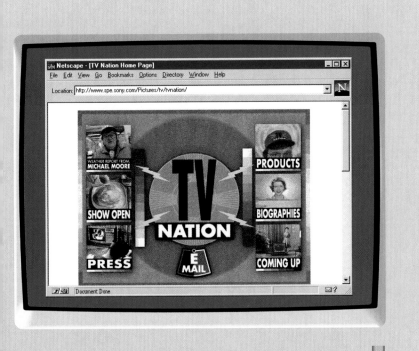

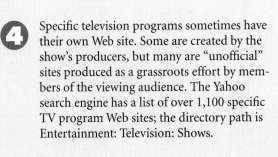

4 Specific television programs sometimes have their own Web site. Some are created by the show's producers, but many are "unofficial" sites produced as a grassroots effort by members of the viewing audience. The Yahoo search engine has a list of over 1,100 specific TV program Web sites; the directory path is Entertainment: Television: Shows.

How to Find Print Media and E-Zine Web Sites

The Internet, especially the Web, is changing the way the public gets its information. Many owners of major publications are no longer in strictly the newspaper business or the magazine business. Instead, they are now finding themselves in the information business, meaning that the public is starting to demand a full range of options, including online resources, for information delivery from commercial sources. The Internet is also opening up a whole new arena of competition for new media sources that focus solely on online delivery, many of which are drawn to the Web for its ability to present information in a graphically rich, interactive, and nonlinear fashion. In short, all the major media companies are realizing the necessity to create an Internet presence.

1 One of the biggest national newspapers also has one of the most extensive Web sites. The USA Today Web site is every bit as bold and colorful as the newsstand version, but since it is on the Internet, this version is updated on a minute-to-minute basis. As in the printed paper, the USA Today Web site contains headline news and photos in the categories of general news, sports, weather, life, and money. The Web site also offers selected links to other online information as well as interactivity in the form of reader response surveys. The URL is http://www.usatoday.com/.

TIP SHEET

▶ Perhaps you are looking for the equivalent of the corner newsstand online with links to all the options listed in this section and more. There are a few excellent resources on the Web that serve just that purpose. One is the Electronic Newsstand at http://www.enews.com/.

▶ A complete resource devoted strictly to e-zines is John Labovitz's E-zine List at http://www.meer.net/~johnl/e-zine-list/. This resource also has a nice synopsis of what e-zines are, with some discussion of their history and future direction.

5 One way to do some one-stop shopping for online magazine and print media sources is to go to the Web site of a megamedia conglomerate like Time-Warner and just click on any one of its many online publications options. This media giant even has its own online service called Pathfinder to help connect you with its varied and substantial offerings. To start at the beginning go to http://pathfinder.com.

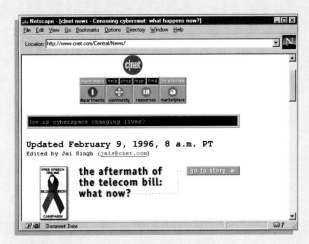

2 c|net Central, one of USA Today's competitors online, has a vast online presence—and it is even reaching out to TV audiences with a new cable television show about the Internet. c|net has up-to-date news and information as well as a whole host of other Internet and Web links and resources. The URL is http://www.cnet.com/Central/News/.

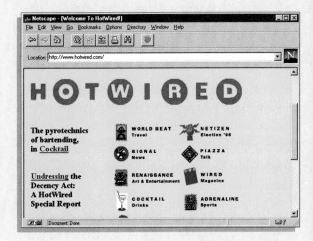

3 The magazines on the Web currently number in the thousands and include everything from online versions of popular print media to purely online e-zines that have no real-world counterpart. One popular newsstand magazine that also offers an extenisve online presence is *Wired* magazine. The wealth of information *Wired* offers through its online site (called HotWired) rivals its colorful and content-rich newsstand version. The URL is http://www.hotwired.com/.

4 An example of a fun and informative e-zine that has no newsstand counterpart (at least not yet) is the Jet Pack online magazine. With quirky eye-catching graphics and an eye for what's happening in pop culture, this online news resource will keep you up to date with all the latest trends and will entertain you in the process. The URL is http://www.jetpack.com/.

How to Find Music Resources on the Web

It used to be that the only musician-related Web pages online were unofficial shrines created by devoted fans. Lately, however, music promoters and music industry professionals are finding that they would like to exert a little more control over the content of their Web presence and are starting to create more and more "official" Web sites for bands and recording artists as an effective avenue for promotion and outreach. And because the Web lends itself to the presentation of multimedia content, it has emerged as a new performance venue in some cases, offering new or hard to find material not always available in the record store.

TIP SHEET

▶ **Most people start their music search by genre. The Yahoo search engine (http://www.yahoo. com) currently has nearly 1,600 Web sites listed by genre in an easy to navigate format. You'll find dozens of genre/style listings sorted alphabetically, from *a cappella* to *world music*. The directory path is Entertainment: Music: Genres.**

▶ **The Web is a good place to find unique or rare musical instruments as well as the people who know how to fix and restore antique or specialty music items. The Web is also the perfect place for finding out about MIDI (Musical Instrument Digital Interface)—a common communications method by which computers produce music—and music software options for using your computer to create, play, and record music. An excellent source serving all these needs is the WWW Virtual Library Music page at http://syy.oulu.fi/music.html.**

▶ ❶ To date there are nearly 8,000 listings for Web sites under the Music category in the Yahoo search engine (http://www.yahoo.com), and this number is growing rapidly. To service this growing demand, a number of Web indices focused strictly on music have emerged. One good one is 1-800 music NOW produced by MCI. This site offers current music industry news and information as well as ways to sample and buy CDs and cassettes online. The URL is http://www.1800musicnow.mci.com/.

❺ The Web can also act as a great level playing field, giving new and emerging artists as much opportunity to be seen and heard as the major stars. One resource devoted to promoting the burgeoning mass of underground music is the Internet Underground Music Archive (IUMA). This is a well-produced resource, with stylish graphics and loads of information about bands you may have never heard of and artist information that you may not be able to find through mainstream music sources. The URL is http://www.iuma.com/.

2 One mega-resource with lots of entertainment links has an extensive section devoted to helping you find music-related information, Web sites, and other Internet sources. The site is called Entertainment Network News, and it has links for every music category, major record label Web sites, and other general music resources. The URL is http://www.slip.net/~scmetro/home.htm.

3 One popular site devoted specifically to rock and roll music is Rock Web Interactive. This site features extensive news and information about various bands and rock artists, complete with promotional material and sound bites from many top performers. The URL is http://www.rockweb.com/.

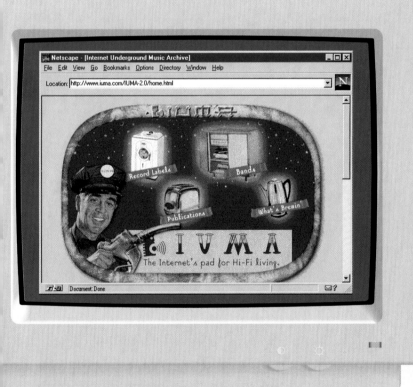

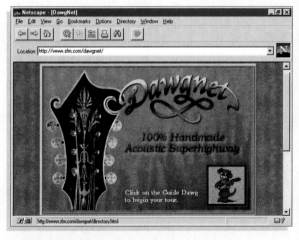

4 A few musicians have their own official Web sites, complete with bios, pictures, audio files, and links to related sites, as well as ordering information for CDs, posters, T-shirts, and so on. Award-winning musician David Grisman commissioned this site to reflect his personality. The URL is http://www.sfm.com/dawgnet.

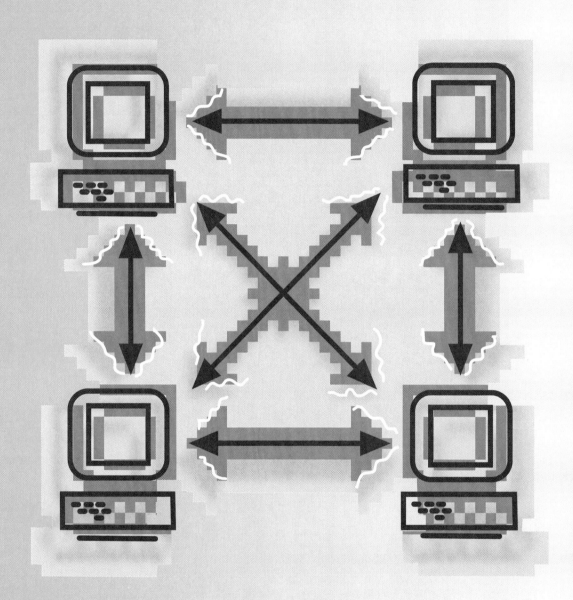

APPENDIX

Resources

 In this appendix you will find some resources to help you in accessing the World Wide Web, as well as some good sites to visit once you are connected.

National Service Providers

America Online
Phone: (800) 827-6364
Fax: none
URL: http://www.aol.co

Arrownet
Phone: (517) 371-7100
Fax: none
URL: http://www.arrownet.com/

BBN Planet Corporation
Phone: (800) 472-4565
Fax: (617) 873-3599
URL: http://www.bbnplanet.com/

CompuServe
Phone: (800) 336-6823
Fax: none
URL: http://www.compuserve.com

Delphi
Phone: (800) 695-4005; (617) 491-3393
Fax: (617) 441-4903
URL: http://www.dash.com/

EarthLink Network
Phone: (213) 644-9500 ; (800) 395-8425
Fax: (213) 644-9510
URL: http://www.earthlink.net/

free.org
Phone: (715) 743-1700
Fax: none
URL: http://www.ferryboard.com/

Global Enterprise Services, Inc.
Phone: (800) 358-4437, ext. 7325;
(609) 897-7325
Fax: (609) 897-7310
URL: http://www.jvnc.net/

Global Network Navigator (America Online)
Phone: (800) 819-6112
Fax: none
URL: http://www.gnn.com/

Greenlake Communications
Phone: (810) 540-9380
Fax: (810) 540-0509
URL: http://www.cris.com/~greenlak/
index.html/

HoloNet
Phone: (510) 704-0160
Fax: (510) 704-8019
URL: http://www.holonet.net/

Hypercon
Phone: (800) 652-2590
Fax: (713) 995-9505
URL: http://www.hypercon.com/

IBM Global Network
Phone: (800) 775-5808
Fax: none
URL: http://www.ibm.com/
globalnetwork/

IPSnet
Phone: (407) 426-8782
Fax: (407) 426-8984
URL: http://www.ipsnet.net/

Imagine Communications Corporation
Phone: (800) 5-MAGIXX;
(800) 542-4499; (304) 292-6600
Fax: (304) 291-2577
URL: http://www.imagixx.net/

Institute for Global Communications
Phone: (415) 442-0220
Fax: (415) 546-1794
URL: http://www.igc.apc.org/

Internet Access Houston
Phone: (713) 526-3425
Fax: (713) 522-5115
URL: http://www.iah.com/

Kallback
Phone: (206) 286-5200
Fax: (206) 282-6666
URL: http://www.kallback.com/worldnet/

LogicalNET Corporation
Phone: (518) 452-9090
Fax: (518) 452-0157
URL: http://www.logical.net/

NETCOM
Phone: (408) 983-5950
Fax: (408) 983-1537
URL: http://www.netcom.com/

Northwest Internet Services, Inc.
Phone: (503) 342-8322
Fax: (503) 343-1699
URL: http://www.rio.com/

NovaLink Interactive Networks
Phone: (800) 274-2814
Fax: none
URL: http://www.trey.com/

PSI (Performance Systems International)
Phone: (800) 82PSI82
Fax: (800) FAXPSI1
URL: http://www.psi.com/

Portal Information Network
Phone: (408) 973-9111; (800) 433-6444
Fax: (408) 725-1580
URL: http://www.portal.com/

Prodigy Services Company
Phone: (800) 776-3449
Fax: none
URL: http://www.prodigy.com/

Questar Microsystems, Inc.
Phone: (206) 487-2627; (800) 925-2140
Fax: (206) 487-9803
URL: http://www.questar.com/

SPRYNET (CompuServe)
Phone: (800) 336-6823
Fax: none
URL: http://www.sprynet.com/

Traders' Connection
Phone: (800) 753-4223
Fax: (317) 322-4310
URL: http://www.trader.com/

Unlearning Foundation
Phone: (408) 423-8580
Fax: none
URL: http://www.netcenter.com/air/air.html

ZONE One Network Exchange
Phone: (212) 824-4000; (212) 824-5000
Fax: (212) 824-4009
URL: http://www.zone.net/

Zocalo Engineering
Phone: (510) 540-8000
Fax: (510) 548-1891
URL: http://www.zocalo.net/

Local Service Providers (Indices)

Mecklermedia: THE LIST
URL: http://www.thelist.com/

Yahoo
URL: http://www.yahoo.comBusiness_and_Economy/Companies/
Internet_Services/Internet_Access_Providers/

Internet Presence Providers (Indices)

NETVIDEO: Web Presence Providers and Designers
URL: http://www.club2000.com/directories/newlist.html

Yahoo
URL: http://www.yahoo.comBusiness_and_Economy/Companies/
Internet_Services/Web_Presence_Providers/

Yahoo
URL: http://www.yahoo.comBusiness_and_Economy/Companies/
Communications_and_Media_Services/Internet_Presence_Providers/

Web Books and Magazines (Indices)

The Unofficial Internet Book List
URL: http://www.northcoast.com/savetz/blist.html

University of Texas: Virtual Computer Library
URL: http://www.utexas.edu/computer/vcl/bkreviews.html

Must-Have URLs

Internet Timeline
URL: http://cgisj.cgi.com/IBC/Timeline.html

Investor Relations—Public Companies
URL: http://networth.galt.com/www/home/equity/irr/publiccoa.html

Fortune 500
URL: http://pathfinder.com/@@tNKlpsFsCQIAQMKI/fortune/magazine/specials/
fortune500/search.html

Hoover's Database of Public Companies and corresponding Web sites
URL: http://www.hoovers.com/search/srch2.cgi

City Net
URL: http://www.city.net/

Nynex Yellow Pages
URL: http://www.niyp.com/

Newslink
URL: http://www.newslink.org/

Virtual Reference Desk
URL: http://www.refdesk.com/

Database For Press Releases
URL: http://www.pressline.com/

Hoover's Online
URL: http://www.hoovers.com/

Reference Desk
URL: http://www.lehigh.edu/~jekd/refs.html

1995 World Fact Book
URL: http://www.odci.gov/cia/publications/95fact/index.html

CREDITS

@Internet Marketing home page reprinted with permission of @Internet Marketing.

Adobe Acrobat Amber screen shots © 1996 Adobe Systems, Inc. Reprinted with permission.

Alamak Internet Live Chat home page courtesy of Alamak Internet. Reprinted with permission.

Aldershot Elementary School home page designed by Bill Doucet's grade 4, 5, and 6 students at Aldershot Elementary School, Kentville, Nova Scotia. Reprinted with permission.

AOL screens © 1996. Courtesy of America Online.

Artline home page © 1995 Haslem Fine Arts, Inc. Reprinted with permission.

Artscope home page © 1996 Artscope, Inc. Reprinted with permission.

The Biz home page courtesy of The Biz, a UK-based business information 'zine published by Easy I LTD—a leading multimedia information publishing and development company. Reprinted with permission.

B'nai B'rith home page reprinted with the permission of B'nai B'rith Interactive.

BrookServe home page © BrookServe. Reprinted with permission.

City Net home page © 1994–1996 Architext Software. All rights reserved. Reprinted with permission.

Claris Web site screen shot used with permission of Claris Corporation. Claris is a registered trademark and Simply Powerful Software is a trademark of Claris Corporation in the U.S. and other countries.

clnet home page reprinted with permission from clnet: the computer network © 1996.

CollegeNet home page © 1995, 1996. Reprinted with permission.

CompuServe screen shots © 1996, CompuServe Incorporated. Reprinted with permission.

Cupid's Network home page © 1996 by Cupid's Network, Inc. Reprinted with permission.

Cybercash home page reprinted with permission.

DigiCash home page reprinted with permission. DigiCash and ecash are registered trademarks.

Digital Campus home page © 1996 Creative Media Generations, Inc. Reprinted with permission.

Doc's Wacky Site home page © doc hbrand. Reprinted with permission.

Emmy Award home page © Academy of Television Arts and Sciences. Reprinted with permission.

ENN/SC Metro online home page reprinted with permission.

Europa home page © 1996 Europa Communications, Inc. Portland, OR. Reprinted with permission.

FAO Schwarz home page © 1995 FAO Schwarz. Reprinted with permission.

Fine Art online home page designed by Danny Brown, edited by Paul Brown. Reprinted with permission.

First Virtual home page © First Virtual, Inc. Reprinted with permission.

Fish Tac Toe applet courtesy of Jason Smith. Reprinted with permission.

Fortune Magazine © Time, Inc., New Media. Reprinted with permission.

GeoCities home page © 1996 GeoCities. Reprinted with permission.

The Hub home page courtesy of the Hub staff. Reprinted with permission.

IMALL home page © 1995,1996 IMALL, Inc. All rights reserved. Reprinted with permission.

Infoseek Guide home page © 1995, 1996 Infoseek Corp. Infoseek, Infoseek Guide, and the Infoseek logo are trademarks of Infoseek Corporation, which may be registered in certain jurisdictions. Reprinted with permission.

Internet Explorer © 1996 Microsoft Corp. One Microsoft Way, Redmond, WA. 98052-6399 U.S.A. All rights reserved. Reprinted courtesy of Microsoft Corp.

Internet Public Library home page reprinted with permission.

Internet Shopping Network home page courtesy of the Internet Shopping Network. Reprinted with permission.

IRC Gallery home page reprinted with the permission of Thomas M. Vestly, a.k.a. "Charge."

IUMA home page © 1995 Internet Underground Music Archive. All rights reserved. Reprinted with permission.

Java home page courtesy of JavaSoft and Sun Microsystems. Reprinted with permission.

JJ Electronic Plaza home page © JJ Electronic Plaza, Inc. All rights reserved. Reprinted with permission.

Kids Page home page reprinted with the permission of Bob Allison.

Lewis & Clark Library System home page © Lewis & Clark Library System. Reprinted with permission.

Meta Info Labs home page courtesy of David Barberi. Reprinted with permission.

Microsoft Network © 1996 Microsoft Corp. One Microsoft Way, Redmond, WA. 98052-6399 U.S.A. All rights reserved. Reprinted courtesy of Microsoft Corp.

NASIRE home page provided courtesy of the National Association of State Information Resorce Executives and should not be used for publication without express permission from the association. Reprinted with permission.

Netscape Navigator screen shots © 1995, 1996 Netscape Communications Corp. Reprinted with permission.

NYNEX Interactive Yellow Pages © 1995, 1996 NYNEX Interactive Yellow Pages. Reprinted with permission.

O'Keeffe-inspired artwork home page © respective owners. Page design © Cortland City School District. All rights reserved. Reprinted with permission.

PC Quote home page © 1995, 1996 PC Quote, Inc. Reprinted with permission.

Portland, OR City Commissioner Charlie Hales's home page reprinted with permission.

Practicing Attorney's home page © 1995, 1996 Internet Legal Services and Peter R. Krakaur, Esq. All rights reserved. Reprinted with permission.

Prodigy screen shots © 1996 Prodigy Services Corporation. Reprinted with permission.

Pronet home page © 1996 Pronet Enterprises LTD. Reprinted with permission.

Public Broadcasting Service home page © 1996 Public Broadcasting Service. Reprinted with permission.

QuoteCom home page © 1995, 1996 Quote.Com, Inc. Reprinted with permission.

Renaissance Internet Services home page © 1995 Renaissance Internet Services. Reprinted with permission.

Rob Hartill's Away Page courtesy of Rob Hartill. Reprinted with permission

Rockweb and Dawgnet home pages © 1994, 1995 Silicon Forest Media, Inc.

Science Tour Demo home page reprinted with permission.

Sci-fi Channel home page used courtesy of USA|Networks—the Sci-fi Channel. All rights reserved. Reprinted with permission.

Seicho home page reprinted with permission.

SeniorCom home page © 1996 SeniorCom. Reprinted with permission.

Shopping Planet home page courtesy of Shopping Planet. Reprinted with permission.

Smithsonian Institution home page © 1995 Smithsonian Institution. Reprinted with permission.

Starwave home page © 1996 Starwave Corporation.

Tektronix home page courtesy of Tektronix, Inc. Reprinted with permission.

TV Nation home page courtesy of Sony Entertainment. Reprinted with permission.

TV Net home page © TV Net. Reprinted with permission.

United Parcel Service home page © 1995, 1996 United Parcel Service of America, Inc. All rights reserved. Reprinted with permission.

University of Texas home page © 1996 the University of Texas at Austin. Reprinted with permission.

USA CityLink Project home page © 1996 Blake & Associates. All rights reserved. Reprinted with permission.

USA Today home page © USA Today, a division of Gannett Co., Inc. Reprinted with permission.

USA Today Weather Page © USA Today. Reprinted with permission.

Web Museum home page reprinted with the permission of Nicholas Pioch.

Whitney Museum of American Art home page © 1996 Whitney Museum of American Art. Reprinted with permission.

World Wide Freelance Directory home page © 1995, 1996 Creativision Publishing Corp. All rights reserved. Reprinted with permission.

WWW Browsers, MIME, and Helper Applications home page © 1995 Douglas C. Tower, University of California at San Diego. Reprinted with permission.

Yahoo! screen shots © 1996 Yahoo!, Inc. All rights reserved. Yahoo! and the Yahoo! logo are trademarks of Yahoo!, Inc. Reprinted with permission.

Yale University home page © 1996 Yale University. Reprinted with permission.

INDEX

Instant **HTML Web Pages**
1-56276-363-6 $24.95

JAVA MANUAL OF STYLE
1-56276-408-X $24.99

HTML 3 MANUAL OF STYLE
1-56276-352-0 $24.99

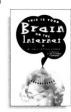

THIS IS YOUR **Brain** ON THE **Internet**
1-56276-356-3 $5.95

Cybermarketing
Essentials for Success
1-56276-328-8 $24.95

Ride the Fast Lane on the Information Highway with Ziff-Davis Press.

net sex
Nancy Tamosaitis
1-56276-285-0 $14.95

ZD PRESS Guide to Netscape Navigator 2.0
1-56276-354-7 $24.99

The latest waves for expert net surfers.

Driving lessons for online newcomers.

http://www.mcp.com/zdpress/

 ZIFF-DAVIS ZD PRESS

Ziff-Davis Press books are available at all fine bookstores or call 1-800-428-5331 to order.